THE HUMAN FABRIC

Unleashing the Power of
Core Energy in Everyone

Bijoy Goswami

with

David K. Wolpert

Aviri Publishing
Austin, Texas

Aviri Publishing
www.aviri.com

P.O. Box 29065
Austin, TX 78755
humanfabric@aviri.com

ISBN 0-9760574-0-9

Library of Congress Control Number: 2004098410

Version 1.1, October 2009

Bijoy Goswami is available for seminars and consulting engagements. For more information, please visit

www.BijoyGoswami.com

ACKNOWLEDGEMENTS

I wish I could list every person who in some way provided me with ideas or inspiration over the years to create this book, but such a list would be too expansive to include here. A few individuals deserve special mention.

I am indebted to Bruce Krysiak for our innumerable conversations which led to the initial formulation and development of the MRE Framework.

My mentor, Martin Henry, provided constant encouragement to accept the task of writing this book.

John Sifonis helped shape my thinking about applications of the Framework for corporations.

Alison Cowden, a truly outstanding editor, continuously took drafts of this book to higher levels of refinement.

Tina Schweiger and her staff at Yellow Fin Studios created a superb cover design and all the illustrations in this book.

Ranjan Goswami, my brother, provided a thorough critique of the book and constructively challenged my assumptions.

Jon Green helped me understand Relaters in a new light and provided assistance in a variety of areas.

In addition, several people reviewed drafts of this book and provided valuable insights and feedback, including Ajay and Kate Agarwal, Girish Altekar, Elizabeth Anders, Alexandra Burrall, Kathryn Carr, Travis Chow, Sara Crowell, Marsh Faber, Hanoz Gandhi, Bryan Hooper, Peter James, Henrik Johansson, Steven List, Darius Mahdjoubi, Lisa Maxwell, Corinne Miller, Cyrus Mistry, Kert Peterson, Asha Prasad, Jeffrey Rovner, Justin Segal, Nancy Stone, Patrick Talley, Matt Wennersten, Chris Yeh, and Matthew Zubiller.

I sincerely appreciate the time and effort all these people generously offered. This book would not have been possible without you, and I cannot thank you enough.

—— *Bijoy*

*For my parents, Leela and Jayant,
and brothers, Shoumitro and Ranjan.
Thank you for your ever-present
love and support.*

— Bijoy Goswami

*For my nephew Eric and sisters,
Karen and Miriam.*

— David Wolpert

CONTENTS

FOREWORD

The Story of the Story

by David Wolpert

Bijoy Goswami understands people in a magical way. He has helped countless friends, business acquaintances, family members, corporations, and even complete strangers understand who and what they are in ways that have had profound effects on their lives. His talent lies in bypassing the mazes of psychologist speak, behavioral theory, organizational behavior, personality assessments, and other structures, and cleanly and elegantly cutting to the root of what is truly important. Converse with Bijoy for a scant three minutes and he can give you insights about you that will leave you wondering why you didn't think of that, or think of it in such a simple, poetic way. Bijoy has spent years developing and continuously refining his model of how people *are* and how they interrelate. Not one to rest on the laurels of simply having it mapped, Bijoy evangelizes his message to anyone who will listen. And everyone does.

I met Bijoy through Sara, a mutual friend of ours. Sara is the consummate Relater. She knows everybody and everybody knows her. When Sara says, "You should get to know this person," she's invariably correct. I would venture that Sara could not articulate how she comes to these conclusions. To her, it's intuition. In the case of Bijoy and me, Sara was right again. He and I clicked immediately. In retrospect, we might not have clicked at all if Bijoy hadn't thoroughly analyzed me within minutes of our first encounter. He had me pegged as an analytical, knowledge-seeking type in no time. Knowing this, he knew that I wouldn't be interested in chitchat. People like me crave ideas. Lucky for both of us, Bijoy had plenty of ideas to share.

Admittedly, at first I found some of Bijoy's ideas dubious. He told me that there are just three types of people—Mavens, Relaters, and Evangelists. What? Just three? Didn't Meyers and Briggs find *sixteen* types of people? Bijoy went on to make a dozen more provocative statements. He claimed, for example, that Mavens working with Evangelists start better companies, and that the roles the three types of people play in society mimics the evolutionary process.

I reckoned that Bijoy was either a quack or was truly on to something. As a Maven, I required some supporting evidence of Bijoy's grand claims. I had a much easier time relating to Bijoy's "Framework" when he pointed out that I was a Maven, Sara was a Relater, and he was an Evangelist. And then I began to think about people like myself, Sara, and Bijoy. I realized there were some compelling consistencies in Bijoy's simple three-tiered categorization. And, indeed, there are numerous examples of how certain combinations of these core types generally do things better.

The more Bijoy talked, the more I ruled him out as a quack. Whatever he was, without a doubt his ideas were intellectually intriguing. I soon came to realize that Bijoy was on a mission. He sincerely wanted to help people however he could, and he clearly believed that his Framework was just the ticket. He told everyone who would listen about it. It did more than help people—it got them excited. It transformed the recipients of Bijoy's ideas into evangelists for his ideas. It didn't take long before people began telling Bijoy to write this stuff down. Until that point, Bijoy had been communicating his ideas in a fragmented form through speeches, white papers, and in one-on-one discussions. What Bijoy needed was a way to capture all the nuances of his Framework in one place, in an organized way. The consensus was that it was time for a book. And that's where I came in. Bijoy thinks best on his feet, talking. I communicate better through writing. A collaborative effort seemed ideal.

I now understand that there is much more to the Framework than a method of classifying people's core being. The real value of the Framework is that it will help you understand that your core type influences your journey through life—how you interact with others and how they interact with you, how well you perform in certain organizations or on certain tasks, and how and why you make certain personal and professional choices. The Framework will even help you understand social phenomena, political and economic issues, and everyday occurrences you never thought could be modeled in a meaningful way.

The Framework isn't going to solve world hunger or achieve a lasting world peace. I do expect, however, that it will make a difference in your life—perhaps just a small difference, but when it comes to understanding yourself and the world around you, any improvement should be welcome.

— David Wolpert

PREFACE

I resisted writing this book despite ample encouragement from my friends. In my mind, the ideas they wanted me to evangelize in a book were not new, and therefore I was not in a position to write about them. Instead, I referred my friends to the many works upon which my "big idea"—the MRE (Maven, Relater, Evangelist) Framework—is based. Some of my friends actually read those works and came back to me with a startling revelation: they felt that I articulated the ideas in a way that made the most sense to them and had the most impact on their lives. In short, they said I explained it better. Jeff Cox, the author of *Selling the Wheel* (one of those books I pointed people to), noted something else. He said that I had a knack for synthesizing many different concepts into an integrated one, articulating patterns and connections that none of those other works identified. My resistance to writing this book thus began to fade.

These factors were the catalyst for my decision to create this book, but another factor gave me momentum. It struck me that while everyone wants to understand themselves better, few people know how. I thought that what people really needed was a simple tool to help them do it. The Framework, I thought, was the solution. Every person I told about the Framework said that it helped them, even if just to a small extent, to understand themselves and those around them better. And that's important, because whether you are building a friendship, a marriage, a team, a company, or *anything* else, people are involved. There is enormous power in being able to relate to people better, and if I had an effective way to do it, I needed to capture it on paper.

But why me? What makes me the right person to pen this book? I believe that the variety and quality of life experiences I have had gives me a unique perspective. In every aspect of my life—spiritual, academic, cultural, and professional—I have found myself crossing boundaries, defying conventional approaches, and combining and integrating dualities, opposites, and extremes. My father is a Hindu Bengali from northern India, my mother an English-speaking Catholic from southern India. After completing third grade in India, I lived in Taiwan for four years and then moved to Hong Kong. In Taiwan and Hong Kong, I attended American schools. As an undergraduate at Stanford, I studied Computer Science, Economics, and History (the mix of which made sense, if only to me). I pursued an honors program in Science, Technology and Society, which helped me weave together the different threads of my academic pursuits. After graduating, I took a job with a software company and tried my hand at product development, technical sales, and business development. I later launched my own software company. And composed music. And wrote a play. And so much more. This combination of diverse experiences in multiculturalism, education, work and play has given me a broad, interdisciplinary perspective on the world. No background could be more appropriate for a book like this.

Perhaps more fundamentally, I'm well suited to write this book because I am passionate about people. I have been called a psychologist, a coach, a guru, a life consultant, and simply a good friend. I possess no formal credentials in these areas, but these are all apt descriptions. For as long as I can remember I have been involved in helping people reflect on their lives. And in all my conversations through the years, one thing repeatedly stands out: without self-knowledge, life is painful and unfulfilling. Individuals must understand themselves in order to find satisfaction and to enjoy and succeed in life. Ancient Greeks visited the Oracle at Delphi to get their fortune told. Inscribed at the gates were the words, "know thyself." The wise Oracle understood that your destiny is inextricably linked to who you are, and knowing who you are would help you meet your destiny. I couldn't agree more.

This is not a book of answers. It's a book of guidance and direction. I am trying to cast you off on a journey of self-discovery. The path of self-discovery is not difficult to follow, but you first have to *find* your path, and it will continuously change. I hope you interpret the ideas in this book not as a rigid and static model, but as a dynamic and organic one. This book is a meditation. It will engage your intellect and your emotion. I will not attempt to exhaustively prove all the claims I make, and the book does have limitations. There's a wonderful adage from George E.P. Box: "All models are wrong, but some are useful." I do hope you will find the Framework useful. But only you can judge if it works for you.

Peace,

Bijoy Goswami

CHAPTER
1

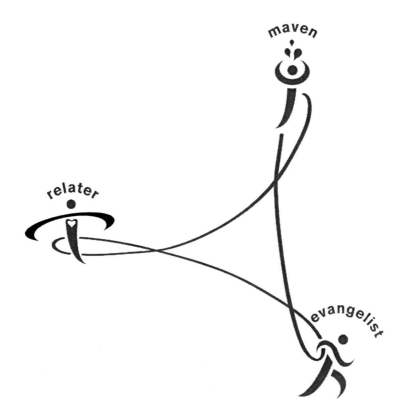

REVISITING THE
GOLDEN RULE

The Golden Rule is one of the oldest human social guidelines. Its simple message of kind reciprocity—to treat others as you would like to be treated—can be found in one form or another in the scriptures upon which virtually every major religion is based, including Christianity, Judaism, Islam, Buddhism, Hinduism, Taoism, and Zoroastrian.

Living by the Golden Rule seems like a sensible heuristic for getting along with others. It provides a simple moral standard by which to evaluate everything we do that affects other people. As such, it's a great starting point for framing moral and ethical decisions. However, the Golden Rule should not be interpreted too literally. Treating everyone as you want to be treated implies that all people are fundamentally similar and therefore want to be treated identically, which we know is not always true. The real essence of the Golden Rule is not so much that we should treat others *precisely* as we want to be treated, but rather that we should try to put ourselves in other people's shoes and appreciate their perspectives. When we do that, we comprehend that individuals are unique and should be treated as *they* want to be treated, which is not necessarily how *we* want to be treated.

The interesting thing is, the Golden Rule's literal interpretation that people are fundamentally similar and would want to be treated just like you is *sometimes* true. You will occasionally encounter individuals who—despite their unique personalities, interests, and talents—resemble you in some fundamental way. Such people are motivated the same way you are and perceive the world around them in a similar fashion. You just "click" with these people. When interacting with them, the Golden Rule applies perfectly. With everyone else, you'll need to try on their shoes. In fact, on average, you'll click with about one person in three.

Getting to the Core

The reason the Golden Rule works so well one-third of the time is that there are fundamentally three types of people, in roughly proportionate counts in the population.[1] The Golden Rule works when *your* type matches that of the other person in question.

By "type," I do not mean personality. Personality is a means of describing outward-facing behaviors—how we interact with others, or act in the presence of others. Tools such as the well-known Myers-Briggs test that assess personalities along multiple dimensions—extroverted versus introverted, for instance—do a good job at describing what you *do* and how you *act*. This is useful knowledge. But such tests fall short in describing what you *are*. This is the definition of a core type: one of three basic human natures, or ways of being. Your core is the underlying *driver* of everything you do. It's the fabric you're made of.

There are three core types: Mavens (M), Relaters (R), and Evangelists (E). That's it—just three! We'll explore each of these core types in detail in the next three chapters. For now, here are the high-level descriptions of the types:

- *Mavens* are knowledge driven. They seek to discover and create knowledge. A quintessential example: Albert Einstein.
- *Relaters* are relationship driven. They continuously strive to create new relationships and deepen the ones they have. For example: Princess Diana.
- *Evangelists* are action driven. They energize others to take action in the world, and also take action on their own. Example: Martin Luther King.

A simple anecdote nicely illustrates how the three core types perceive the world differently. You have probably heard the adage, "It's not what you know, it's who you know." Relaters would agree with that statement. From their perspective, it really is about *who* you know. Mavens, conversely, do believe it's all about *what*

---

[1] Throughout this book I make many bold, unsubstantiated claims. This book is not derived from a rigorous sociological study. Rather, it is based on my own experiences, observations about people, the study of various religions, and the readings of several authors. I encourage you to challenge my statements. The Appendix lists many of the works on which my thinking is based.

you know. Evangelists need their own saying, because for them it's about what they can make happen.

Before I go any further, I need to make a confession: I didn't invent this notion of a three-tiered classification system for describing people. The concept that there are three core types is not new. In fact, it's *really* old. The ancient Indian spiritual text *Bhagavad Gita* explains that people take three paths, or *yogas*, in life: Jnana, Bhakti, and Karma. Respectively, these are the yogas of intellect (Maven), devotion (Relater), and action (Evangelist).

Much more recently, Malcolm Gladwell's book *The Tipping Point: How Little Things Can Make a Big Difference*, identifies three types of actors involved in the spread of what he calls "social epidemics:" the Maven, the Connector, and the Salesman. Gladwell defines Mavens more narrowly than I do because he discusses them in a very specific context, though I give him full credit for naming Mavens so appropriately. "Connector" is an appropriate term, but I feel Connectors must *relate* to people before they can connect them together. The term "Salesman" is not quite right for my purposes because, as I will explore in Chapter 4, Evangelists aren't always about selling things.

In her book, *"I Wish I'd Said That!": How to Talk Your Way Out of Trouble and Into Success*, Linda McCallister outlines six communication styles, three of which she calls "dominant": Noble, Reflective, and Socratic. She explains that people with different communication styles use communication for different purposes. The Noble (Maven) uses communication to convey truth, the Reflective (Relater) uses it to deepen relationships, and the Socratic (Evangelist) uses it to persuade.

First, Break All the Rules: What the World's Greatest Managers Do Differently, Marcus Buckingham's book, explores the differences between talents, skills, and knowledge. He asserts that while skills and knowledge can be acquired over time, talents are innate and cannot be learned. And guess what? Buckingham discovers three categories of talent: thinking (the Maven), relating (the Relater), and striving (the Evangelist).

When you put these models together, the overlap is apparent (Figure 1). McCallister focuses on communication styles; Gladwell focuses on affecting widespread social change; and Buckingham focuses on the relationship between talents and effectiveness in a business environment. None of these authors generalize their observations to reflect a person's *total way of being*—your fabric. This fabric encompasses how you communicate and how you shape change, how you learn and become motivated, and indeed how you live life itself. McCallister, Gladwell, and others describe individual strands of this fabric. My intent is to weave those strands together and present it in a way that has tangible value to understanding yourself and others. To phrase it ambitiously, I aim to construct a grand unified model for understanding human nature. I call this the MRE (Maven, Relater, Evangelist) Framework.

	Bhagavad Gita	The Tipping Point	I Wish I'd Said That	First, Break All the Rules
Maven	Intellect	Maven	Noble	Thinking
Relater	Emotion	Connector	Reflective	Relating
Evangelist	Action	Salesman	Socratic	Striving

Figure 1:
Different Elements of the Core Types

The Framework consists of two components. First, it contains a model for classifying people into one of three types, and for understanding the relationships between people of different types. Second, it contains a four-step prescription for how to understand and analyze the core types, which will be discussed in Chapter 5. In short, the Framework is a model of how people are, plus a recipe for what to do.

My attempt to classify ways of being is not a purely academic pursuit, nor is it part of a religious or philosophical quest. On the contrary, I want to help you understand yourself and others better so that you can realize very practical benefits. My goal here is not to answer all your questions about people and life. All the answers you need are within you; I simply want to help you find those answers. It all begins with understanding people's core nature.

The Pattern of Three

There's something intriguing about the use of three terms to describe our core natures. The *Bhagavad Gita* describes the three paths that people walk in life; Malcolm Gladwell describes three types of people involved in spreading social epidemics; Linda McAllister identifies three dominant communications styles; and Marcus Buckingham describes three types of talents. Hinduism provides another example: the notion that there are three Godheads—Brahma, Vishnu, and Shiva—that represent the three human-like manifestations of God: one who creates, one who preserves, and one who destroys.

Thousands of years of history have demonstrated that there's some recurring significance to three when describing human nature. Why three? It helps to think of the many ways to characterize people as a continuum. On one extreme, one could argue that all people are fundamentally the same; as John F. Kennedy eloquently stated, "There is more that unites us than divides us." On the other extreme, one could argue that all people are truly different, giving us six billion types. That's a pretty big range. Between those extremes, you often hear adages that there are just "two types of people in this world." What are those magic two? Perform an Internet search on Google for the phrase in quotations, and you'll discover over five thousand pairings. There are also constructs like the Enneagram model, which divides people into one of nine categories, and the Meyers-Briggs test, with sixteen types. Clearly, a smaller number of classifications can be more readily grasped, while too large a number of classifications is too complex to be applicable in a daily context. But again, why does the number three, in particular, work so well? Why not four or five?

The answer might lie in evolution. Charles Darwin (a Maven) observed that the evolutionary process has three general steps. First, there is variety. At some point, there are innumerable, slightly different versions of the same basic organism. There might be, for instance, a dozen varieties of a specific fish, each with seemingly irrelevant minor differences between them. Next, there is selection. One or two things that once seemed irrelevant ultimately prove to be critical in the game of survival of the fittest. The one variety of fish with a color pattern that turns out to be camouflage to predators flourishes, while the bright red fish that signals "come eat me" to sharks slowly becomes extinct. Finally, we have retention. The superior camouflaged fish reproduces prolifically while the other varieties slowly die out.

These three steps of evolution are analogous to what Mavens, Relaters, and Evangelists do in everyday life. The interactions of Ms, Rs, and Es in some way mimic the evolutionary process (though of course no one becomes extinct). The variety phase of evolution is analogous to what Relaters do. Relaters typically have lots of variety in their personal connections; some connections are shallow, some deep, some are useful, some not, some make sense, and some don't. Relaters revel in the variety of fish that were in the early oceans. Mavens select. They pick and choose their friends and their allies and make every major decision in their life with intent and analysis. A Maven knew before anyone else did which fish was best suited to survive in the long run. Finally, Evangelists run with a good thing when they see it. Their mission is to spread the word that one particular fish is going to thrive. There are Ms, Rs, and Es in the human genetic mix precisely because nature has found that this is the mix that works best.

Understanding the MRE Framework

The Framework is more than the assignment of a category to every person. As you read through this book, the complexities of the Framework will become apparent. A few points are worth making up front.

No one is an absolute M, R, or E. That is, nobody fits perfectly into one of these core types. This is one of the differences between the Framework and the other three-tiered classification systems mentioned earlier, all of which place people exclusively into one type. However, every person is *predominantly* one of the three types. Think of the Framework as a triangle, and the core classification as a sliding scale between two points on the triangle, as shown in Figure 2. The scale moves along only one edge of the triangle. You will often encounter people who are combinations of types along one edge, such as M-R, R-E, or M-E.

The balance between these two types varies by person, but every person is grounded as only one type. For example, you might be 60% Maven and 40% Evangelist, but this means you are a Maven. It is difficult to precisely assess the composition of an individual's fabric, and it is not important to do so. Whether someone is 60/40 or 70/30 or 55/45, the point is that the predominant type wins out. Can someone have a perfect 50/50 mix of two types? The answer is no. The Framework is based on a premise that all people are primarily driven by one of three things: knowledge, relationships, or actions. To have a 50/50 between core types would imply that someone is equally driven by two of those three things. This would be one severely conflicted individual.

It's tempting to affix overly simplistic labels to the types, such as Mavens are "smart," Relaters are "social," and Evangelists are "persuasive." Likewise, it's tempting to conclude the inverse: that Relaters and Evangelists are not smart, that Mavens and Evangelists can't relate to people, and that Mavens and Relaters can't convince anyone to do anything. This is not the case. Being smart, being social, or being able to persuade really have nothing to do with the core. It's a subtle but important distinction: the core is not about *what* you do, it's about *why* you do it. We all do the same basic things, but people of each of the core types do them for different reasons.

Let's revisit the issue of how a core type is different from personality. It might help to think of a core type in terms of what you would be if there were no people with whom to interact. As a thought exercise, consider a situation in which you suddenly find yourself on a deserted island. In this situation, characteristics of your personality really wouldn't matter; it's hard to "act" extroverted, for example, when you're the only person around. If you're

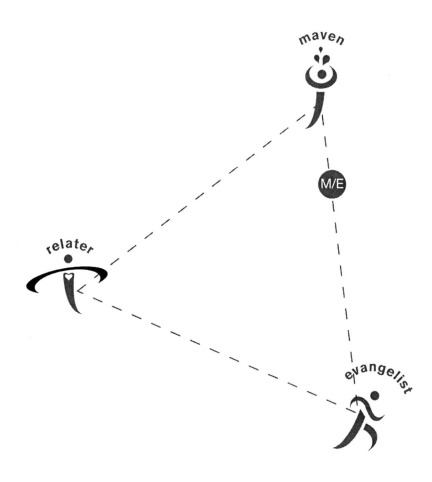

Figure 2:
The MRE Triangle

a Maven, you will try to make rational sense of what's happened to you and attempt to think yourself out of this mess. The extreme Maven might actually enjoy the intellectual challenge of making sense of this. Evangelists, in contrast, will skip the analysis and take action. While the Maven will be reflecting on what to do here, the Evangelist will be off looking for people and building a shelter. He's not inclined to sit and reflect, even when there's time. The lone Relater will be pretty unhappy in this situation. He might seek companionship from other animals or give a "human" face to inanimate things, just as Tom Hanks' character did with Wilson the volleyball in the movie *Cast Away*. The point is that one's personality varies depending on who is around you, whereas your core type is static. It does not change whether you're with one person, a hundred people, or no people at all.

It is important to keep in mind that the M, R, and E designations are not inherently good or bad. However, there is a darker side to each one. Mavens can become hopelessly self-centered and make terrible collaborators. Relaters can befriend the wrong people and be manipulated. Evangelists can become so focused on advancing their ideology that they lose touch with the truth. We'll explore the dark sides of the core types in the next three chapters.

It bears repeating: your core is not about what you say or do—it's about why you do it. I am an Evangelist (20% Maven), yet most people assume I am a Relater because I have a vast network of friends and business acquaintances. Those who perceive me as a Relater misunderstand the Framework. I don't have a large network because I'm driven at my core to connect to people just for the sake of it; rather, I have a large network because I have found a way to catalyze the people in that network into agents of action for me. Mavens, Relaters, and Evangelists all leverage what they have or can obtain to get the outcomes they desire. Remember, the issue to explore is *why* people do what they do, not *what* they do.

Now, even though a core type has nothing to do with how we act, we can get some clues about our core type by observing behavior. To understand how this is possible, consider dogs. Have you ever thought of a dog as smart? Don't some dogs just seem to be able to figure things out or remember things better than others? And then there are the ultra-empathetic dogs, which possess an uncanny ability to "tune in" to human emotions and convey concern and compassion. We also have the alpha dog—determined, stubborn, the leader of the pack. It's remarkable that not only do dogs possess the same core types as people, but that we can discern their type without language-based communication or demonstrations of specific skills. The Maven dog can't analyze data, the Relater dog can't introduce us to other dogs, and the Evangelist dog can't persuade us to do *anything*, but nonetheless we can usually figure out their type by noticing, for example, which dog leads the pack. Behavioral evidence alone is not necessarily conclusive, but it can be a useful tool to assessing core types.

What's Next

I've thrown out a lot of ideas in this chapter to lay the groundwork for further exploration of the Framework. At this point, I suspect that you have some combination of emotions: excitement, curiosity, confusion, skepticism…maybe you want your money back. What you feel will depend largely on your core type. Here's a perfect opportunity to highlight some differences among them.

If you are a Maven, you won't be completely satisfied at this point because I haven't addressed every imaginable issue. You want data, proof, examples, and a thorough rebuttal of all potential counter-examples. You already have a list of questions percolating in your mind. You most likely have objections to my discussion of the Golden Rule, which was intended merely to be thought-provoking. I hate to say this, but you probably won't find this book completely satisfying because I can't prove every assertion I make. However, the Appendix includes a list of readings which can provide some background to help you form your own opinions.

Relaters, you should be pumped. At last, those crazy Mavens and Evangelists will understand your actions and intentions. At last, they'll comprehend why you call them all the time to say nothing in particular. They'll understand why you are a walking directory of people and just how valuable that is. It's finally making sense to them, right? Well, almost. They'll have to finish the book first. Encourage them to do so.

You Evangelists are my new best friends, because you're going to tell all your friends to read this book. (Thanks!) Now, of course, you will want to transform the messages in this book into actions. You're going to take notes as you read this and make little reminders to yourself to try this and that. I won't discourage you, but be patient. You will be applying some of these ideas tomorrow, but be careful, because as Evangelists come to learn, a little knowledge can be a dangerous thing.

Whatever your core type, you'll get something useful out of this book. The next three chapters will discuss Mavens, Relaters, and Evangelists in depth, with lots of examples for our Maven friends. Chapter 5 will provide some tools to help you identify your core type. Our exploration of the Framework is not limited to individuals. Corporations have core types, too, which are detailed in Chapter 6. Chapter 7 shows how to use the Framework for setting better political, economic, social, and educational policies.

My ultimate goal here is to equip you with the skill to apply the true meaning of the Golden Rule—to treat others as *they* would want to be treated. The first step is understanding the three core types in detail.

Enjoy the ride.

CHAPTER
2

MAVENS

1. Introduction

The Wright Brothers are generally credited with inventing the airplane, but they didn't. Fixed-wing, powered aircraft from inventors around the world were developed years before the legendary flight at Kitty Hawk. The problem was, all these planes either never got off the ground or crashed immediately upon takeoff. The Wright Brothers' real achievement was not the invention of basic aircraft design, but rather the means to *control* flight. They introduced the elegant concept of control in three axes (pitch, roll, and yaw) and built the first mechanical controls to safely maneuver an airplane using those principles. They invented a highly efficient propeller to solve the challenges of sustained lift and propulsion. They built a revolutionary aluminum engine with no spark plugs or carburetor. They also pioneered the principles of modern flight testing and built the first wind tunnel. The Wright Brothers essentially invented the entire field of aeronautical engineering.

This was no small feat for anyone to achieve, but on the surface the Wright Brothers seemed like particularly unlikely individuals to identify what the real obstacles to flight were and to find a solution. Neither Wilbur Wright nor Orville Wright attended high school, and neither of them had any training in mathematics or any other supporting field which might have proved useful. Both brothers initially pursued careers in the printing business and later made custom bicycles. So how did they come up with controlled flight?

In 1920, Orville gave a deposition in a court case. The defendant's counsel asked him, "When and under what circumstances did you and Wilbur Wright first become interested in the problem of flight?" Orville's response:

> "Our first interest began when we were children. Father brought home to us a small toy actuated by a rubber spring which would lift itself into the air. We built a number of copies of this toy, which flew successfully. By 'we' I refer to my brother Wilbur and myself. But when we undertook to build

15

the toy on a much larger scale it failed to work so well. The reason for this was not understood by us at the time, so we finally abandoned the experiments. In 1896 we read in the daily papers, or in some of the magazines, of the experiments of Otto Lilienthal, who was making some gliding flights from the top of a small hill in Germany. His death a few months later while making a glide off the hill increased our interest in the subject, and we began looking for books pertaining to flight. We found a work written by Professor Marey on animal mechanism which treated of the bird mechanism as applied to flight, but other than this, so far as I can remember, we found little.

In the spring of the year 1899 our interest in the subject was again aroused through the reading of a book on ornithology. We could not understand that there was anything about a bird that would enable it to fly that could not be built on a larger scale and used by man. At this time our thought pertained more particularly to gliding flight and soaring. If the bird's wings would sustain it in the air without the use of any muscular effort, we did not see why man could not be sustained by the same means. We knew that the Smithsonian Institution had been interested in some work on the problem of flight, and, accordingly, on the 30th of May 1899, my brother Wilbur wrote a letter to the Smithsonian inquiring about publications on the subject..."[2]

Orville and Wilbur were playing with what was essentially a prototype of a helicopter back in 1878—over sixty years before helicopter technology became viable. And they didn't just play with the toy, they studied it and built their own versions of it. They began to research similar things, like how birds fly. And they remained persistent in their exploration. They weren't doing this for profit. They just found it fascinating.

---

[2] Deposition in *Regina C. Montgomery et al. v. the United States, January 13, 1920, in* The Papers of Wilbur and Orville Wright: Including the Chanute-Wright Letters and Other Papers of Octave Chanute, *2 vols., ed. Marvin W. McFarland (New York: McGraw-Hill, 1953), 1:3.*

The Wright Brothers aren't unique. In fact, some of the greatest scientific and technological advances of the last century came from surprising people. Albert Einstein never studied physics in school, and Thomas Edison had no experience with any of the things he invented or perfected. It is beyond the scope of this book to address the myriad of reasons why these individuals were able to do what they did. What they had in common, though, is that they were all driven by the same overarching motivations: the pursuit of knowledge. They were all Mavens.

2. It's All About Knowledge

Mavens seek to order the world through their intellect. They are driven to acquire, synthesize, and create knowledge. Mavens are hard-wired to actively seek out information and then find ways to apply and cross-reference their newly acquired knowledge. The Wright Brothers learned a lot about the basics of flight from a toy, learned about machinery from their work at a printing shop, and later learned about the importance of balance and control in a custom-built bicycle. While Relaters and Evangelists might not always connect the dots, Mavens can't help but do so.

For a Maven, all knowledge is potentially useful. This is not to say that Mavens find *everything* interesting. But Mavens do tend to find a wide range of things interesting, because the greater the diversity of knowledge a Maven has, the larger the foundation he has on which to construct new knowledge or figure things out.

To see this in practice, observe a Maven play in a trivia tournament. Watch what happens when the Maven doesn't know the answer outright. He will come up with a best guess by drawing on a large and diverse pool of information. What country did Celine Dion represent in the Eurovision contest held in Dublin in 1988? Dave Wolpert, who helped me write this book, knew a little about the French language, geography, and pop culture, and reasoned it out this way: Celine is a French name, Celine speaks with a French accent, Celine is extremely popular in Canada, so Celine might be French Canadian, but the Eurovision contest is only open to European nations, only three countries in Europe speak French,

France and Belgium have a lot of national pride and probably wouldn't allow a Canadian contestant to represent them, so maybe Celine represented Switzerland, which would make sense because Switzerland has never had an internationally recognized pop star. Dave's guess of Switzerland was correct.

Mavens are information sponges. Additional knowledge makes the Maven's model of the world around him more rigorous. To this end, Mavens stay on top of current events. Many Mavens will ritualistically watch television news programs, read newspapers and magazines, visit data-intensive websites, and subscribe to multiple e-mail newsletters. My friend P.J., a Maven, likes to read the skillfully written stories in *The Economist* as much as I do. But he starts reading from the back pages—the ones chock-full of economic facts and figures. In a professional work environment, Mavens like to read as many reports as they can get their hands on and attend as many informational meetings as possible. In short, a Maven cannot get too much information. On the contrary, the risk is never getting enough. A Maven finds *not* knowing things to be emotionally unsettling. Mavens fear being "the last person to know" or having information withheld from them. Some Mavens find decision- making based upon incomplete information to be unbearably stressful.

As sponges, Mavens don't just absorb knowledge—they also "squeeze it out." Malcolm Gladwell calls Mavens *information brokers*. Indeed, Mavens seek a two-way exchange of knowledge. Mavens soak up as much knowledge as they can, but they also derive intrinsic satisfaction from disseminating it, especially to other Mavens who have similar intellectual interests. Relaters and Evangelists should understand that Mavens revel in using their minds to help others. As a result, Mavens are often labeled as helpful people; they might be, but their motivation for helping others runs deeper than the explanation that they're just kind and considerate. Mavens truly enjoy sharing knowledge. It's instinctual and therapeutic for them to do so.

3. Innovation and Creativity

Mavens are prolific distillers of ideas. They absorb vast amounts of information from multiple sources, analyze it, and then formulate new concepts. Mavens apply a mixture of linear thinking (A leads to B leads to C) and a web, or matrix, of thought. The power of the Maven is his ability to take volumes of unrelated data and formulate something new and constructive out of it. Maven inventors like Thomas Edison and the Wright Brothers are sometimes considered tinkerers—people who invented amazing things by trial and error, sweat and persistence. That's partly true. But, the more things Edison invented, the more he learned about other technologies and about the creative process. Edison did more than invent a few hundred things: he invented a *process* to invent a few hundred things.

Unlike Evangelists and some Relaters, Mavens are not creative in the sense of developing completely new ideas in a vacuum. Einstein's Theory of Relativity, although groundbreaking, was based on the contributions of hundreds of mathematicians, physicists, and other scientists throughout history. Mavens excel at evaluating the strengths and weaknesses of existing concepts from disparate areas to make something new. The Wright Brothers combined their knowledge of bicycle manufacturing and the mechanical complexities of print shops to make an aircraft capable of controlled flight. In another interesting example, in 1948 a Swiss inventor named George de Mestral found himself covered in burrs after walking his dog in the wilderness. Curious as to how the burrs stuck to his pants, he put one under a microscope and found that its surface comprised small hooks that effectively clung to the small loops in the fabric of his velour pants, similar to how crochet works. This metaphorical combination of *vel*our and *cro*chet was the genesis of Velcro.

This brings us to an important recommendation for Mavens: cross-pollinate your ideas! Insight comes from unexpected places—from daily life, from other people, from areas of interest not related to yours. The key is always to be open to new things coming into your world. This process can take a long time. In 1968, a research scientist at 3M inadvertently stumbled on a new kind of adhesive that was sticky enough to latch on to things securely and yet could be detached and re-applied repeatedly. The scientist, Spence Silver, didn't know what to do with his invention. The adhesive found some limited use in other 3M products five years later, but it wasn't until a man named Art Fry tried to solve an out-of-left-field problem that Post-It notes took off in 1980. The problem? Art Fry wanted a bookmark for his church hymnal.

As a Maven friend of mine was once told, "You take a helicopter view of the world, which allows you to swoop down into the trees and yet soar above the forest." Mavens who realize they have this power can capitalize on it.

4. Decision Making

Mavens are highly detailed decision makers. Data-driven and analytical, Mavens will thoroughly investigate an area of interest and will diligently examine options before reaching a decision. Mavens make lists of pros and cons. They construct spreadsheets for comparing options. They read product reviews—all of them—before buying anything. As such, Mavens can be great shopping consultants. A Maven car expert, for instance, could help a Relater or Evangelist friend interested in buying a new car to narrow down a list of suitable candidates and apply some objective criteria to choosing the best one for her friend's needs.

Mavens occasionally struggle with understanding others' decision making styles and motivations. Take car shopping, for instance. Mavens evaluate cars based on objective criteria such as price, fuel efficiency, horsepower per liter, and 0-60 acceleration time. Tell a Maven you want the best sports car available, and he might recommend a Chevrolet Corvette—an excellent suggestion from a purely numerical standpoint. But Evangelist and Relater buyers will have one big objection: it's a Chevrolet. Had the Maven recommended a Ferrari, Maserati, Lamborghini or Porsche, that recommendation might be well-received. But a Corvette just doesn't have the image, style or sexiness of an exotic European sports car. Many Mavens will struggle with this notion of buying a car for image. While intellectually they understand that image plays a role in a purchase decision, most Mavens will find it silly that some people would pay so much more for something that offers, on paper, so much less. The Maven would miss the point that a sports car (or a house, or clothes, or many other things) appeals to one's emotions as much as or more than one's intellect.

By the way, if you are a Relater or an Evangelist reader, keep in mind that by nature Mavens find reasons that things will *not* work. Do not go to a Maven for encouragement on a new idea. Instead, go to the Maven for a critical analysis of it. You will be rewarded with a thorough analysis of your idea, with particular emphasis on potential trouble spots. Knowing those pitfalls can help you plan better and minimize risks.

5. Communicating

Mavens differ in how they value the importance of communicating their ideas to others. Mavens will usually only communicate when they have something meaningful to say or, when Mavens seek to acquire new knowledge, they will engage in exchanges from which they believe they will get knowledge back. Einstein was a prolific letter writer. He frequently corresponded with many of the great European physicists, who helped him develop his theories. Conversely, Mavens will avoid conversations where it is unlikely that knowledge will be traded. This is why Mavens loathe nonchalant conversations and chit-chat, unless it is simply intended as a prelude to a more involved knowledge exchange.

Mavens tend to speak with precision and completeness. Refer back to Orville Wright's deposition at the beginning of this chapter. Orville, like most Mavens, goes out of his way to avoid ambiguity. Even when it is generally clear in context that when Orville is talking about a toy brought to "us" by his father he is referring to himself and his brother, Orville still finds it necessary to clarify that, "By 'we' I refer to my brother Wilbur and myself." Orville also adds details that are not relevant, such as his reference to gliding flights from the top of a small hill in Germany—does it matter that the hill was small, or that is was in Germany? Though such details are not important, they do serve to present a complete picture of the facts. For a Maven, this is important.

In conversations, Mavens will generally acknowledge when they don't know something, but they might handle this in different ways. Some Mavens will state that they simply don't know the answer to a question, for example, but then re-shape the conversation toward what they *do* know. In other situations, a Maven might jump on this opportunity to learn something completely new and ask the other person to tell them all they can—"I've never heard of that, but it sounds interesting. Can you fill me in?"

You can often spot a Maven in a group discussion if he wavers between intense interest when one subject is discussed and complete withdrawal when another is broached. While Relaters enjoy the simple act of communicating regardless of topic, Mavens require substance for the discussion to be enjoyable. If the topic of conversation is shallow, the Maven has nothing to gain and will disconnect from the conversation. You can always re-engage a Maven by asking his opinion, especially on a topic that you know he will find interesting.

Mavens are single-taskers (as opposed to multi-taskers) in two respects: in how they think, and in how they speak. For a Maven, these two tasks, or processes, run parallel but are closely linked. Mavens require focus when speaking and generally prefer to address one topic at a time. This is because the Maven brain is hard-wired for depth, not breadth. A Maven cannot speak on multiple issues concurrently because she cannot think about multiple issues in depth concurrently. Furthermore, for a Maven, the speaking process *is part of* the thinking process. Nothing is worse for a Maven than to be interrupted when he is waxing eloquently. It is important to understand that *Mavens do not stop thinking, even while talking.*

Mavens prefer modes of communication with the least emotional content. Phrased differently, Mavens prefer communications with substantive content (signal), not laden with pleasantries, emotional issues, or chit-chat (noise). This high signal-to-noise ratio requirement explains why Mavens love e-mail and detest long personal phone calls. With e-mail, a Maven can quickly skip non-essential text and zero-in on the important content. Then, a Maven can take time to plan a response and word it effectively. The signal to noise ratio of most phone calls is low, and the Maven is under uncomfortable, continuous pressure to respond quickly.

6. The Internet: A Maven Wonderland

The Internet has had a profound effect on the way people interact. I realize that the Internet is only used by a small percentage of the world's population, and even in the most technologically-savvy societies Internet usage isn't quite mainstream. However, the trend toward increasing adoption of the Internet is clear and unstoppable. Even those who do not regularly use the Internet are aware of its impact and are affected by it. The Internet has had different implications for Mavens, Relaters, and Evangelists.

The Internet might be the best thing that's ever happened to Mavens. The Web is essentially a gigantic index of information, and Internet tools like e-mail and instant messenger applications allow a Maven to collect and disseminate knowledge efficiently. To highlight a few examples:

- Customizable Web portal sites like My Yahoo or iGoogle allow a Maven to pick only the snippet-sized content in which she is interested and view it in one integrated screen.
- There are hundreds of sites that feature reviews of everything under the sun—books, movies, music, cars, lawnmowers. This allows Mavens to filter the good from the bad based on quantitative data and qualitative opinions from millions of people around the world.
- Search engines allow a Maven to find whatever information he needs. Google is particularly well-suited to Mavens because of its customizability; users can limit their searches, for example, to sites in a particular language or only those relevant to their geographic location.

- Online dating and social networking sites allow a Maven to find and evaluate people based on searchable parameters, such as age or favorite movies.
- As mentioned earlier, e-mail allows a Maven to prepare carefully crafted correspondence. And although instant messaging applications can interrupt a Maven's work, they can also be useful tools for sending or receiving small amounts of information quickly.
- Mavens use the Internet as a virtual clipping service for their friends. For instance, my friend Darius knows my areas of interests well and will go out of his way to scour the Internet for articles that he knows I will find interesting and e-mails them to me.

7. Relating to Others

In building relationships, Mavens seek out other Mavens. Mavens set a high standard for those they will allow into their world. Invariably, they find that most people simply do not measure up. Of the three core types, Mavens have the hardest time relating to others. While high on IQ (intelligence quotient), they are lowest on EQ (emotional quotient). It's sometimes hard for the Maven to cloak his disdain for others who are not deep thinkers. It's frustrating for Mavens not to be able to find more people with a similar intellect. Mavens might therefore be perceived as arrogant (and of course some are). Mavens develop mechanisms to deal with the reality of not being able to interact with more Mavens on a daily basis—arrogance, aloofness, or sarcasm.

Mavens usually need large blocks of uninterrupted time to work on the things they're passionate about. Einstein developed many of his theories while working at the Patent Office in Switzerland. Through not intellectually engaging, this job afforded him plenty of time to think.

Mavens like in-person interactions the least because of the amount of emotional exchange that usually occurs with those conversations. However, Mavens do enjoy in-person exchanges with other Mavens. Attend any technology conference and you'll see what I mean; I call these "Maven fests."

8. Persuasion

Aristotle identified three types of persuasion (yes, another triad!)—*logos, pathos,* and *ethos*—which map nicely to Mavens, Relaters, and Evangelists, respectively. Logos is an argument based on logic and reason. Pathos is an emotionally based argument. Ethos is an argument based on the credibility and reputation of the person advancing it.

Evangelists are generally the most persuasive of the three core types. Mavens can be very persuasive, too, but their source and style of persuasion are very different. An Evangelist persuades with her personality, passion, and energy. An Evangelist will instill trust; you will want to do what an Evangelist wants you to do because you will find the Evangelist trustworthy and her passion contagious—an *ethos* type of persuasion.

In contrast, a Maven persuades only with the intellectual rigor of her argument—a *logos* type of persuasion. A Maven might exude no passion whatsoever about her ideas, but she will try to convince you with the elegance and completeness of her argument. You might disagree with her position, but it is hard not to consider it carefully. Furthermore, a Maven's arguments come across as honest and well-intentioned, not pushy in a slick salesperson way. Mavens can thus be good salespeople, but only for things in which they truly believe (I will discuss the specific issue of sales abilities in Chapter 6). They're not proficient at dishonesty.

As you can imagine, this means that Mavens can be particularly persuasive in certain situations but not necessarily in others. Consider the different kinds of debates. In the kind of debate held in high school competitions, the winner is selected by the persuasiveness of his arguments; specifically, how well he researched the topic and articulated a case built on facts. Mavens generally do well in such a situation. But in a Presidential debate, where there is no designated winner, the public and the media will evaluate the

debate not by the specific arguments made or facts cited, but rather by the overall personal effectiveness demonstrated by the
candidate. In this situation, Evangelists (and many Relaters, too)
really shine. You might recall that in the 1984 presidential campaign, Walter Mondale, a Maven, tried to make age a campaign
issue in his favor against the older Ronald Reagan. A highly talented Evangelist, Reagan deflected Mondale's attack with the brilliant line, "I refuse to let age become an issue in this campaign. I
will not use my opponent's inexperience and youth against him."
Mondale later said he lost the election at that moment.

Mavens are effective debaters against other Mavens. Mavens
see "debates" with other Mavens more as a discussion with an
intent to solve a problem than as an all-out verbal battle. Mavens
welcome dissenting viewpoints because these are opportunities for
a Maven to re-examine his own thinking and strengthen his arguments, if not simply develop effective rebuttals to those who do
not agree with him. Any debate between two Mavens will leave
both Mavens happier. Each will hear good arguments, giving each
other new insights on the opposing viewpoint. Each Maven will
then leverage that new information to strengthen his position, or
take on an entirely new position. Either way, the Maven would
view that outcome as successful. The more "pure" Mavens (80+%
Maven in their fabric) see debate as a conflict to be avoided, whereas Mavens with a healthy dose of Evangelist in their fabric might
be highly effective debaters against anyone.

It is important to understand that one critical difference between Mavens and Evangelists is the goal of their persuasion.
Evangelists attempt to persuade because they want others to take
action. The Maven's goal is to convince others of the "rightness"
of his argument but not necessarily to take action on it. You often
see this in practice with Maven politicians who can articulate a
problem and a solution effectively, but stop short of implementing
their own solution or encouraging others to do so.

In the year 2000, I was discussing search engines with my
friend Bruce, a Maven. Back then, there were quite a few search
engines on the market, and Google was a relative newcomer. In
the middle of our discussion, Bruce quietly mentioned, "I use

Google." I didn't think much of it at the time. A week later, Bruce noticed my frustration with using other search engines. "What's the problem?" he asked me. "These search engines!" I blurted out. "None of them work! I keep having to click 'next 10' to get what I want!" With a little more emphasis than Bruce's normally calm demeanor, he exclaimed, "Dude, I told you to use Google!" Once I tried Google, I loved it and have never used another search engine since. I liked it so much, in fact, that I went on an Evangelist crusade and convinced everyone I knew that they should use it, too.

This example nicely highlights the difference in persuasion and communication style between Mavens and Evangelists. When Bruce told me a week prior that he used Google, in his mind he was recommending that I do, too. But I took his comment as nothing more than a data point—Bruce uses Google. Remember, Mavens don't pick a preferred *anything* for no good reason. The subtext of what Bruce was telling me was, "I have evaluated all the search engines, and Google is the best, and therefore everyone should use it." Bruce actually thought that's what he communicated to me. When talking to a Maven, keep in mind that almost everything they state as an opinion or observation is actually a recommendation.

9. Career Choices

Mavens are generally happiest in roles incorporating large doses of analysis, strategy, data, and quantitative computation. Many Mavens gravitate toward the science, engineering, mathematical, statistical, and computer-related professions. Mavens also typically pursue careers as:

- Financial, industry, and other types of analysts
- Educators in more technically focused fields and at higher levels (college-level business more frequently than middle school English, for example)
- Consultants, especially strategic consultants

- Researchers, journalists, investigative reporters, and detectives
- Sales and marketing professionals of technical products
- Linguists
- Doctors, especially surgeons
- Accountants
- Lawyers

These are the fields in which Mavens feel the most comfortable. This does not mean, of course, that these are the only fields in which you will encounter Mavens, nor is this to say what Mavens *should* do. Mavens can be fine nurses, for instance, but if you think about the best nurse or any kind of caregiver you've ever had, he or she was probably a Relater.

It is all too easy to stereotype Mavens as "technical types." You will find Mavens in every field. Leonardo Da Vinci was a Maven. Most people regard Da Vinci as a great artist. But he was also a self-educated mathematician, architect, inventor, and engineer. He frequently combined his studies in one subject to improve his understanding of another. For example, Da Vinci dissected human bodies to study their shapes so he could paint them better. He invented crude forms of photography and copying— five hundred years ago. And, believe it or not, Da Vinci tried to build his own flying machine after studying birds and bats. He even once built a wind-up helicopter!

Salvador Dali was most likely a Maven, too. His art became progressively more complex over time, filled with subtleties, hidden cues, double meanings, and political and religious statements. Escher, too, was probably a Maven. His art was all about puzzles for the mind. Da Vinci, Dali, and Escher all exhibited a sort of logical approach to their art. To be sure, they were all extremely talented artistically and their art can be embraced and enjoyed purely on its aesthetic merits. But there is a reason that so many scholars have studied the Mona Lisa, and entire books have been written to reveal Dali's intentions. These artists didn't just paint for the sake of painting; there was calculation and deliberateness in their work.

There are of course other types of artists whose Maven-ness isn't conveyed directly through their works. Consider, for instance, the musician Sting. His widely acclaimed music, taken alone, wouldn't necessarily support that; it's great music, but many Relaters and Evangelists produce great music, too. But watch or read an interview with Sting, and you'll agree that he's a Maven. In fact, Sting has been criticized for being *too* intellectual about his music. Sting has said that for him, making music is like figuring out a jigsaw puzzle. He also loves to put obscure references in his songs, such as the reference to Nabokov in his song, "Don't Stand So Close to Me." Sting has also said that when pitting himself against rivals for a woman's affection (he's married now), he usually degrades his rivals for their lower IQs.

The exploration of the core types is not about outcome, it's about process. These examples of Mavens are meant to drive home the point, once again, that the key issue with core types is not about *what* but rather *how*. All these Mavens do different things, but their approaches are similar and they do them for the same underlying motivations.

10. Telltale Signs of a Maven

There is no one simple test to determine whether you or someone you know is a Maven. But there are a few signs that might help you make this determination. In general, Mavens are:

- Interested in a broad spectrum of things from an intellectual perspective
- Passionate about things that capitalize on their depth of knowledge
- Known for great ideas, but not necessarily for action
- Detail-oriented
- Good writers, particularly for technical or business writing which requires logical and linear organization
- Articulate speakers
- Love to debate, and are good at it
- Eager to help others make decisions

- Energized at making sense out of vague or incomplete information
- Tend to socialize with other Mavens

The most important question to ask yourself to determine whether you really are a Maven is *What energizes you the most?* Take any point above and frame it as a two-option choice. Do you get energized by knowing a wide range of things (breadth), or do you find it more satisfying to know a lot about only a few things (depth)? Can you passionately write an intellectually-focused paper, or do you find it more enjoyable to write creatively?

11. The Evolution of the Maven

I mentioned in the first chapter that one could "become better" at their core type. Your core type is largely innate, and we all start off at what I would call a "young" level. Young, in this context, doesn't equate to age—it's more analogous to a level of understanding of who and what you are. Not everyone progresses to the next level, which I call "wise." A wise Maven realizes the limitations of a Maven and actively works around them. There is no way to map out the entire process of transformation—or evolution—of a young maven to a wise one. Everyone's path will be different. But a few examples might help to spur your thinking on this.

All Mavens perceive the source of their power to be knowledge. A young Maven believes that, since power is good, knowledge should be protected. At some point in your career you probably encountered a Maven who knew everything about something and wanted to keep that information to himself. Many view that as a means to secure their job. A wise Maven, in contrast, knows that sharing knowledge is actually *more* powerful. The "know-it-all" is really only useful if he can help others to know it all, too.

As another example, a young Maven undervalues the importance of Relaters and Evangelists. Mavens are very good at seeking out other Mavens for whatever they need. Young Mavens believe that other Mavens can provide everything they need. But wise

Mavens know that Relaters and Evangelists are natural complements and can provide so much more, as I'll explore in Chapter 5.

12. The Dark Side

Your strengths are your weaknesses. Each of the three core types has their own unique set of challenges, which I call a dark side. Perhaps the most significant challenge a Maven faces is the inability to take action. Mavens are by nature great at identifying problems and formulating solutions, but are often poor at implementing them. A Maven can retreat into a cave of ideas. For example, in the world of entrepreneurship, Mavens often correctly identify important business problems that are in desperate need of a solution. A Maven may come up with an elegant idea for a company to tackle that problem, and might then go on to develop an ironclad business plan to launch that company. More often than not, however, that company will fail if the Maven tries to launch it alone.

Part of the problem is that Mavens often fall victim to the trap of analysis paralysis—conducting so much analysis that a decision never gets made and action never gets taken. Mavens often feel that they never have sufficient information to make a decision and thus resist making one. A Maven entrepreneur, for example, might research a prospective market without end, focusing on crafting the perfect business plan instead of on launching a company. It is telling that for all the Wright Brothers did to advance the aircraft industry, little became of their own aircraft company. It usually takes an Evangelist to push the Maven into action. Thomas Edison launched several companies, but he had a large component of Evangelist in his fabric. At another extreme, Da Vinci collected so much information that he didn't know what to do with it. He is well known for the many projects he abandoned, and for the numerous journals he left behind, filled with unrealized drawings and ideas.

Another factor against taking action is that Mavens often underestimate the value in collaborating with others who can help them. They might retreat into their world of ideas and away from people. Mavens believe that *what* one knows is the only basis for succeeding in the world. A Maven might therefore not see the value Relaters and Evangelists bring to the table in a collaborative situation. Relaters believe the basis for success is *who* one knows, and for the Evangelist the issue is what one can *do*. This is why many successful companies are launched with two or three people—one person is the idea man (Maven), one has a golden Rolodex (Relater), and one can sell products to or raise money from anyone (Evangelist).

Mavens also tend to underestimate the importance of communication. They tend to assume that what they know is intuitively obvious to Relaters and Evangelists, and thus reason that additional communication would be redundant. In the corporate world, Mavens often belittle the importance of major news for employees and investors. In March 2004, Sir Philip Watts, the CEO of Royal/Dutch Shell, did not deem it important to personally convey to employees and investors that four billion barrels of oil that it thought it had might not actually exist. Understandably, the company's stock price tumbled drastically, yet Watts resisted overcommunicating to alleviate concerns and continually dismissed the news as a "technical adjustment." This kind of undercommunication problem leads to another one: Mavens often believe that if people know what they know, they'll know what to do. Maven managers therefore do not always give clear marching orders or set expectations appropriately to those who work for them.

Another pivotal challenge Mavens face on a daily basis is that they might carry their intellectually oriented decision making too far, especially when it comes to something as illogical as human emotion. Mr. Spock, the character in the original Star Trek series (or his *Star Trek: The Next Generation* counterpart, Mr. Data) epitomizes the extreme Maven mentality. Spock is ruled by logic and perceives emotion to be the enemy of logic, and thus an inferior way to make decisions or carry on life. Mavens might struggle with a decision such as whether to propose marriage or break up with a significant other because they will be compelled to base that decision, to some extent, on purely logical criteria. Psychologists often have to point out to Mavens in therapy sessions what Relaters and most Evangelists know intuitively: emotions aren't logical, and sometimes people do things without good reason, or without any reason whatsoever.

I'll revisit the Star Trek analogy in the next few chapters. It turns out that the roles of characters on all the Star Trek television shows are carefully balanced combinations of Mavens, Relaters, and Evangelists. The "mix of three" phenomenon introduced in Chapter 1 produces great teams and appeals to viewers. Great writers perpetually explore the tensions between the ways different types of people perceive the world—and the conflicts and comedy that result when these types clash. Would the television show *Friends* have been such a great show without the Maven character of Ross? In the next chapter I'll discuss the Deanna Troi's and Rachel Green's of the world—the Relaters.

CHAPTER
3

RELATERS

In the last ten years, Jon Green has worked for six technology companies in various management roles. The longest time he was between jobs was a mere two weeks, even during tough economic conditions. Jon's secret to continuous employment is simple: he makes keeping in touch with people who might someday lead him to a new job a part of his daily routine. By doing so, he keeps abreast of which companies might need his skills before a job opening is posted, even when he is currently employed. More importantly, his personal contacts at these companies give him preferential consideration for any new openings. This strategy is not revolutionary; career consultants have espoused this for years. Even so, not everyone can do this as well as Jon can. The people that do it best are of the second core type: the Relaters.

What is completely intuitive to Relaters like Jon is the value of personal relationships. He understands that relationships need to be nurtured, and nurturing requires continuous attention. Jon has lists (some mental, some on paper) of people with whom he wants to keep in regular contact. He might diligently call one particular person every Monday, for example. Jon doesn't call these people for any particular reason. He doesn't have an agenda. If something interesting is happening in his life, he will of course share it. But if not, he's perfectly fine discussing the weather, sports, business, politics, or whatever else is interesting to the person with whom he is speaking. The topic isn't important. What's important is that he's making a connection.

When a Maven or Evangelist says he "knows" someone, he might only mean that he knows that individual's e-mail address, or that they've spoken once or twice, perhaps years ago. Relaters' concept of "knowing someone" is much deeper. Relaters know what the people in their network have been up to much more recently. Ask Jon what every person he's worked with in the past five years is up to today, and Jon could probably tell you with stunning accuracy. Even if Jon hasn't talked to you directly, he's talked to people you know who have filled him in on what's happening in your life these days. Relaters pay attention to the details that Mavens and Evangelists might consider trivial: people's birthdays, the names of spouses and children, favorite sports teams, and so on. These pieces of information help a Relater nurture a relationship by framing discussions in a more personal context. "How are Chris and James doing?" is a more connective question than "How are your kids?" More personalized questions reflect a higher level of interest and empathy.

It follows that Jon is sought after to fill positions in which he manages relationships. His current position with an electronics manufacturer requires him to fly around the world building relationships with partner companies. He's not selling, designing, negotiating, or building anything tangible. He's not managing a specific product, nor is he managing people. He's building and managing relationships. If something goes wrong in the alliance between two companies, Jon finds a graceful way to resolve it. But when things are going right, as they do most of the time, Jon's whole focus is on making new connections, and transforming existing connections into stronger ones.

It's All About Relationships

Relaters interpret the world around them in terms of people and relationships. They are perpetually driven to create new relationships while deepening the ones they have. Relaters are not particularly interested in knowledge, yet relate to people much as Mavens relate to knowledge. A Maven "connects the dots" between disparate pieces of data to construct new realms of knowledge. A Relater studies individuals and their relationships with others to construct a holistic picture of their personal network. Just as Mavens like to talk about their intellectual topics of interest, Relaters enjoy talking about the people they know. For a Maven, the mysteries of the universe are the ultimate puzzle. For the Relater, people are the puzzle.

The Relater's focus on people permeates all of her interests. For example, Jon loves Formula One car racing. Although the Maven side of Jon is intrigued by the technology of the cars, what really fascinates him about car racing is the people in the sport.

Jon tells you about the personalities of the drivers, the skills of the crew, and the strengths of entire teams. In a similar fashion, Relaters study the personalities and skills of actors in a movie, or the musicians in a band.

Highly empathetic individuals, Relaters understand people intuitively and effortlessly. (Think of Doctor McCoy of the original *Star Trek* series, or Counselor Deanna Troi from *The Next Generation*.) Much more so than the other core types, Relaters are attuned to what I call *context*. While Mavens focus on knowledge and Evangelists focus on action, Relaters focus on everything *about* people—their mood, their "energy," body language, tone, and how they are feeling. Take the example of a business lunch meeting. Regardless of the specific topic discussed, after lunch each of the three core types will reflect primarily on different things: a Maven will reflect on what he learned (about the company and business details), an Evangelist will reflect on action (opportunities and next steps), and the Relater will reflect on everything about the person with whom he met ("he'd be a good guy to work with"). Relaters aren't so much interested in what Bob said, but rather *how* he said it and what they learned about Bob as a result.

The most obvious sign that someone is a Relater is that you feel at ease with them the moment you meet them. Because Relaters live in the realm of emotion they can break down barriers and instill trust. Bill Clinton, who is in part a Relater, exemplified this with his often quoted phrase, "I feel your pain." Whether he did or didn't, people believed him, and it made them feel immediately comfortable and "connected" to him.

Relaters are nurturers. This explains why Relaters often pursue careers as nurses, social workers, counselors, psychologists, and teachers. You might be wondering, then, whether most Relaters are women. I cannot cite an empirical study to support this, but from my own observations I think the answer is an unequivocal yes. I would speculate that at least 60% of women are Relaters, versus perhaps 20% of men. The most reasonable explanation I can offer for this is that nature has seen to it that mothers have many of the qualities that define Relaters—empathy, intuition, and patience.

Relaters are keenly observant of how those around them interact with each other. They are natural experts at interpersonal dynamics. In a meeting or in any other group situation, Relaters take notice of individuals' competing agendas and evaluate their underlying motivations for actions and words spoken. This study enables Relaters to help others to find common ground and reach consensus. Relaters are thus natural diplomats.

Demystifying Relaters

There is often confusion about what Relaters actually are. Various personality assessments and literary works have interchangeably called them Connectors, Socializers, Nurturers, and other terms. Let's dispel two myths right now.

First, Relaters do not necessarily know a lot of people. Most do, but this is not a prerequisite for being a Relater. Mavens and Evangelists might know a lot of people, too, but this point alone obviously doesn't make them Relaters. Some Mavens and Evangelists I know have large numbers of connections, and some Relaters I know have very small networks. For a Relater, the quality of relationships is much more important than quantity.

Second, Relaters are not necessarily social. They can be surprisingly introverted. You might imagine that Relaters frequently attend huge parties with lots of friends and can talk up a storm. Again, some do, but not all. Relaters are actually at their best when interacting with a single individual or with a small group.

Relaters, as I define them, are best characterized as empathetic individuals. They read people effortlessly and relate to them effectively. This ability to relate to people allows Relaters to do something else: connect people. Just as a Relater can intuitively relate to another person one-on-one, so too can the Relater identify individuals or groups that would benefit from knowing each other, and the Relater is happy to make those introductions. These two talents are related but distinct.

Relating: Getting to Know You

Relaters build relationships without a particular goal in mind. Whereas Mavens and Evangelists have a deliberateness about whom they seek to connect to (Mavens seek out people through whom they can gain or share knowledge; Evangelists seek out people whom they can inspire to take action), Relaters have no specific aim. A Relater does not assign a value to relationships with specific people. Instead, a Relater sees all links with people as potentially beneficial—perhaps not immediately and perhaps not in a critical way, but nonetheless all people in the Relater's network can play a useful role. Relaters appreciate that every interaction with a person is a chance to make a friend, learn something new, secure a future job offer, find a customer or business partner, or just help someone out. Whether any reciprocal value is actually realized is of secondary importance.

The important issue is not the quantity but the quality of the connections. When a Relater says, "I know that guy," he means that he knows that person *well*. Furthermore, when a Relater says he "knows" someone, the statement comes loaded with implications. Relaters do not stay close to people they do not respect, nor introduce others to such people. Implicit in saying "I know him" is the notion that the Relater respects him and is willing to stake his reputation on facilitating an introduction or endorsement.

When Relaters meet someone new, they construct a mental diagram to highlight how they and other people overlap with shared interests or a common situation. They will lead with the usual roster of non-intrusive questions, such as "Where are you from?" This helps establish the *context* by which they will relate to someone. Relaters gain clues about you from subtle things such as the adjectives you use to describe your background or the amount of emotional content in your answers. Again, context is more important to a Relater than content.

Relaters build relationships slowly. They take a step, wait for the other person to take a step, and so on. This way, the relationship is built together. The Relater's approach is similar to the way business is conducted in most Asian nations, where the initial focus is always on establishing a personal relationship with people they intend to do business with before delving into business matters. This cements trust. Importantly, the Relater is not compelled to lead people and their fledgling relationship in a specific direction. Rather, the Relater seeks to help individuals find the best path for themselves.

Relaters have a complex circle of trust. For a Relater, nothing is more important than the trust he places in others. How Relaters utilize this is apparent in how they make decisions such as big-ticket purchases. Relaters will first survey people they count upon for input, or simply rely on what their trusted sources have done as examples for what they should do. If a Relater wants to buy a new car, for example, the first thing she will do is ask her sources what they think she should buy, or examine what they drive. This circle of trust applies to business relationships, as well. Relaters will have a strong preference to do business with those they trust, regardless of any objective criteria such as price. This is in stark contrast to how a Maven operates. A Maven, of course, would conduct his own analysis of what car to buy or whom to do business with, basing his decision primarily on purely objective criteria. A Relater sees the entire universe as subjective, whereas a Maven sees it as objective. For a Maven, competencies are always more important. For a Relater, the relationship is paramount, and even a weak personal bond is better than no bond at all.

Relaters view violations of their trust as unforgivable. Once the bond of trust is broken, the relationship might be forever unsalvageable. In addition, Relaters seek—and need—the approval of others. They need to feel validated. Even though Relaters have a natural tendency to like everyone, they have no place in their lives for those who are selfish, cruel, or do not maintain integrity because these people provide them with no positive validation. To some extent Relaters can therefore be the most judgmental of the three core types.

Connecting Others

Relaters, by nature, excel at understanding people. Their innate ability to relate to others forms the foundation of their core. As Relaters gain wisdom and experience in relating to others, they begin to uncover another latent talent: the ability to connect people.

Making connections strengthens the Relater's standing within her network. It positions the Relater as someone who knows the right people. It is the Relater who bridges the gaps between Mavens and Evangelists and enables Mavens and Evangelists to do the things they do best. Ultimately, without the right people, the knowledge of Mavens and the visions of Evangelists would come to naught. This puts Relaters in a position of enormous power as introducers and matchmakers. While Relaters relate to an individual on a one-on-one basis, they connect to many.

Relaters are consummate networkers, yet their approach to networking is not overt. Relaters generally do not attend formal networking events because they consider *every* event or chance encounter to be an opportunity to network. For a Relater, such forced attempts to connect people are superficial and ineffective. Formal networking is a Maven's or Evangelist's way of attempting to emulate what Relaters do naturally.

Relaters match people based on the perceived compatibility of their energy levels—for example, high- versus low-energy people, or people who lead fast versus slow lifestyles—and do not rely solely on objective criteria. It's not that Relaters necessarily think person A should meet person B because they can do something for each other. Rather, it's that A complements B and therefore they might be valuable to each other. Relaters intuitively believe something good will emerge from these pairings, although they are rarely sure precisely what.

Some Relaters intentionally assemble a group of dissimilar people to take part in something the Relater enjoys. Jon, for instance, frequently invites eclectic mixes of people to attend music concerts, one of his passions. Jon can then actively facilitate introductions and conversations between people who otherwise would never have met. As Jon says, "These are some of the most reward-ing matches of all for me because I feel that everyone's horizons are broadened as a result of learning more about different kinds of people."

Relaters are generally not detail oriented when it comes to in-formation. An interesting consequence of this is that some Rela-ters don't pay close attention to what people know or do. They latch on to limited descriptors of people—"he's in healthcare"—and use that anchor as a way to connect others. This often leads to "false introductions." The person "in healthcare" might actually sell health insurance and thus not be particularly interested in meeting surgeons. While this can be awkward, the result might be good: Relaters introduce people to each other who otherwise might never have met.

Communicating

Linda McAllister writes that for Reflectives—her equivalent of a Relater—the purpose of communication is to maintain and ad-vance a relationship. Linda calls them Reflectives because they mirror the energy, pace, style, and tone of conversation of the people with whom they're communicating. Better than the other core types, Relaters adapt their communication style to the prefe-rences of the receiver. There is thus no one consistent Relater style. For examples, Relaters are sensitive to the fact that Mavens in their network generally prefer e-mail to phone conversations and will thus adapt to that.

Relaters do not communicate in a linear fashion. They know that magical things are revealed in the course of an unstructured conversation. This is why Relaters have little interest in structured meetings with agendas—they prefer to simply let the conversation flow in whatever direction it takes. There does not need to be a point or goal to the conversation. It does not even matter who is present. Relaters find ways to make any meeting—on any topic, with anyone—rewarding for its participants.

Within minutes of meeting a new person, a Relater will determine what you and he have in common and use that as a starting point to advance the relationship. Everything you say is interesting to him because every piece of communication helps him understand you better. The content of the conversation is secondary to the relationship that percolates from the discussion. It's analogous to a book club. The purpose of a book club is about personal interaction; discussion of a book merely provides a context. This ability to quickly find a topic of mutual interest and to synchronize communication styles enables the Relater to have a more meaningful interaction with others.

Relaters prefer modes of communication that best facilitate the sharing of emotion. One-to-one, in-person interactions are thus preferred. Relaters realize that you cannot really know someone without personal interaction. A phone conversation would be their second choice. A cell phone is a Relater's best friend, because it enables her to communicate with her network at any time. E-mail and written correspondence are the Relater's last resort for communication because these media have little to no emotional content and might even unintentionally convey the wrong emotional message. Relaters shy away from an over reliance on technical means of communicating because they believe that relationships cannot be automated. For a Relater, "knowing" a person requires physical contact, in part because observing body language is one way Relaters come to understand others. Relaters need to look you in the eye.

Relaters communicate effectively through more "channels" than Mavens and Evangelists. For instance, you can access a Relater's world by listening to her music. Every song by Sarah McLachlan evokes an emotion—loss, sadness, joy, desire, or love. All her songs deal, in one way or another, with relationships. Her lyrics are poetry. Her rhythms and arrangements are frequently unconventional. Even her song titles reveal her Relater-ness: "Fear," "I Love You," "I Will Remember You," and "Sweet Surrender," to name a few. It's not just her words which transport the listener into the world of emotion. It's the very quality of her music, her voice and way of expression.

Relaters are not known for their persuasiveness. In fact, Relaters generally avoid confrontational discussions because Relaters perpetually seek harmony and are generally unassertive. Relaters frequently use qualifiers to soften the impact of their statements and rarely speak in absolutes. As a result, a Relater will rarely persuade a Maven or Evangelist. However, Relaters can very effectively persuade other Relaters, or Mavens and Evangelists with a large portion of Relater in their fabric. Relaters trust Relaters. Relaters' source of persuasion is *pathos*, an emotionally based argument. This means Relaters can be very persuasive about things such as convincing others to donate time or money to a charitable organization.

Innovation and Creativity

The source of inspiration for Relaters' innovation and creativity is people and emotion. Their innovation stems from brilliantly and incisively exploring the emotional realm. This is perhaps why most artists, of every genre, are Relaters. The reason that their art appeals to people is precisely because it "connects" to their emotions. However, Relaters are not Maven-like in their mastery of knowledge and, as such, are generally not great inventors of things. Relaters live in the realm of possibility. In contrast to Mavens, who want to reduce a sea of choices to the optimal one, Relaters enjoy swimming in the ocean of ideas. As a result, Relaters tend to be superficial in their knowledge of things in the world. They possess breadth, not depth. Bringing back Darwin for a moment, Mavens are good at selecting from a sea of ideas, but it is the Relater who creates the set of choices from which Mavens select.

It's easy to find examples of well-known Mavens and Evangelists. Western society celebrates Mavens' inventions, and historians dedicate their lives to studying the great Evangelists. It's comparatively more difficult to quickly conjure up the names of famous Relaters, in part because Relaters tend to live in the background. Even so, Relaters are *everywhere* in the artistic world. They dominate the world of art—whether it be music, poetry, painting, sculpture, or any other form. Art accesses our emotions, and therefore who better to create art than someone who intuitively understands emotions? This works two ways. Good artists can access you, and through their art you can access them. Many artists will tell you that creating art helps them access their own emotions, too.

Relaters are also everywhere in the business world. Have you ever heard of Mike Markulla? Mike was the *third* person who helped get Apple Computer off the ground. If you're in the business or technology world, you probably thought there were only two people (Steve Jobs and Steve Wozniak), didn't you? Steve Jobs, an Evangelist, is hard to forget. Steve was not particularly technical but saw an untapped market for easy-to-use personal computers. Jobs needed Steve Wozniak, a brilliant Maven engineer, to make the Apple computer a reality. The story of how Jobs and Wozniak built Apple Computer is legendary. But Mike Markulla? Mike, a Relater, was an experienced technology marketer. He understood the computer business, knew the right people to make things happen, knew how to sell, invested his own money into the fledgling company, and knew how to attract more capital, based on his connections and his credibility. Without Mike, Apple probably never would have become what it did. You sometimes have to look hard to find Relaters, but they're everywhere.

A Special Role for Relaters in Organizations

Interpersonal friction inevitably results when organizations reorganize, merge, are acquired, or have layoffs. During any kind of structural change, employees worry about losing their jobs, being forced to abandon work they were passionate about, reporting to a new boss, or being asked to relocate, among other disconcerting possibilities. Relaters can play an important role in such chaotic times by bridging gaps between groups and helping turn "them" into "us." Organizations should embrace the natural ambassador qualities of Relaters to ease transitions and mend differences.

In the event of two large companies merging, I would suggest that key Relaters in both organizations be given an unrestricted budget to network the two organizations at a deep personal level, however they see fit. For a geographically dispersed organization, they should be given an unrestricted travel allowance, too. By establishing and fostering new relationships, Relaters will naturally break down barriers and steer the company toward successful integration.

The Limits of Being a Relater

Relaters' extreme attachment to people in their world blinds them from knowing when to scale back or abandon a relationship. Relaters can develop a mindset which over-values relationships and connecting so much that they will connect even when the relationship is causing a negative impact on their lives. Many Relaters remain in painful or unproductive personal relationships, or stay in jobs they dislike out of a sense of loyalty.

Another challenge for Relaters is that they can be so relationship oriented as to be ineffective when asked to perform tasks that are more conducive to Mavens and Evangelists. For example, if a Relater is given the kind of work assignment a Maven craves—go lock yourself in a room, analyze this and that, and develop some recommendations—a Relater will struggle. Activities that emphasize intellect over emotion, or activities that require independent work over group work, can be painful for Relaters. In the workplace, this can cause Relaters to be viewed as professionally ineffective in companies that value tangible output like reports and analyses.

The communication style of Relaters is another significant challenge. Relaters can be so soft-spoken and unassertive that their comments are ignored by Mavens and Evangelists.

What's Next

The world would be an interesting place if there were only Mavens and Relaters. We would have an abundance of great ideas and in-depth analyses, coupled with people who really know people. Returning to the *Star Trek: The Next Generation* analogy, we would have a bridge crew of the android Mr. Data and Deanna Troi. Missing from this mix are people who leverage *what* Mavens know and *who* Relaters know to make things happen. We need Number One, Commander William Ryker. Prepare to enter the world of the Evangelist.

CHAPTER
4

EVANGELISTS

"Are these the beginnings of profound changes in the Soviet state? Or are they token gestures, intended to raise false hopes in the West, or to strengthen the Soviet system without changing it? We welcome change and openness; for we believe that freedom and security go together, that the advance of human liberty can only strengthen the cause of world peace. There is one sign the Soviets can make that would be unmistakable, that would advance dramatically the cause of freedom and peace. General Secretary Gorbachev, if you seek peace, if you seek prosperity for the Soviet Union and Eastern Europe, if you seek liberalization: Come here to this gate! Mr. Gorbachev, open this gate! Mr. Gorbachev, tear down this wall!"

Ronald Reagan
West Berlin, 1987

Part I: The Big Picture

L et's cut to the chase: *Evangelists make things happen!* They are guided by five principles:

1. There is always a cause.
2. Life is about action.
3. Communication is about persuasion.
4. Knowledge is only useful if practical.
5. Relationships are opportunistic.

There Is Always a Cause

It's easy to recall some great causes in history: the notion that all people, regardless of their race, are equal; the pursuit of democracy and political freedom over tyranny; the wrongness of slavery; the national effort to put a man on the moon before the end of the decade; and today, the war to defeat terrorism. Causes on this grand scale were spearheaded by strong Evangelists.

Evangelists are adventurers who constantly embark on new quests. They find a cause that impassions them and make it their own. Paul, one of the early proponents of Christianity, traveled through Judea to spread "the good word." Before he became a proponent of Christianity, Paul used to persecute Christians. It was his mission in life to suppress the nascent religion and all its adherents. He experienced a dramatic conversion in the desert, after which he spent the rest of his life converting people to Christianity. Paul remained the same before and after his conversion experience—he was an Evangelist to the core who simply switched causes! It is due to Paul's significant influence that the path to salvation lay in "good works" or actions, which Evangelists deem the most important. For an Evangelist, one's actions do speak louder than words! (Luther, a Maven, later challenged this notion and came up with the notion of "justification by faith alone.")

Of course, few Evangelists evoke wide-scale political change or propel new religions. Evangelists do not generally care about the scale of their cause. Most of the causes for which Evangelists fight are more subtle, day-to-day things—some of which unexpectedly turn into monumental successes, even if that wasn't the intention. It's Michael Dell believing that he could make a personal computer better than IBM did. It's FedEx founder Fred Smith's conviction that he could deliver packages anywhere in the world within 24 hours, a feat that the Post Office and the United Parcel Service never thought possible. It's Bono, the lead singer of the rock band U2, who has used his popularity at various times to increase awareness about the war in Northern Ireland and encourage African debt forgiveness. It's the software product manager who believes that her prioritization of customer product requests is the right one. It's the restaurant critic who believes that one particular restaurant is hands-down the best one on earth. Causes can be negative, too; a vocal Evangelist disgruntled by a bad customer service experience, for instance, can be a company's worst nightmare. Evangelists are anyone who believes with unswerving commitment that their cause, whatever it is, is worth pursuing and that their approach to realizing their cause is unequivocally the right way to do it.

Life is About Action

Sure, Mavens and Relaters might have causes, too. The difference is that the Evangelist feels an uncontrollable urge to transform his beliefs into tangible actions. Believing in something is not enough.

Evangelists are consummate multi-taskers. They seek—and need—*constant* activity. Evangelists always have an agenda. They want everything to happen "right now" and have little patience for those who slow them down. It's not surprising, then, that Evangelists are comfortable making decisions quickly and with highly imperfect information. They shoot first and ask questions later. In fact, Evangelists thrive on making decisions under pressure. They find it thrilling. The flip side to this is that while Mavens suffer from analysis paralysis, Evangelists frequently suffer from not analyzing situations enough. This is why, as I'll explain in Chapter 6, Evangelists benefit from the balance of a Maven by their side.

Whether it's about a recent book they've read, a movie they've watched, or a product they love, Evangelists have *strong* opinions and are constantly foisting those opinions on others. They take an extreme stance on any topic—and will often take a position they don't necessarily agree with, just to be controversial. Evangelists love nothing more than a good argument. It's a way of crossing swords and tangling with others, which is an Evangelist's way of getting to know someone. Much to the chagrin of the Relaters and Mavens who correspondingly argue from emotion and a sense of rightness, respectively, Evangelists see debate as sport. Rarely will they back down from a good argument.

You will know when you've met a strong Evangelist. You'll feel like a wave of energy has hit you. You'll be inspired and energized to do something. You'll want to learn more, stay close to them, and do what they say. It's like a drug addiction: you want to keep coming back for more and just can't seem to get enough. Of course, some Evangelists can overpower the tolerance levels of Mavens and Relaters—there is such a thing as an overdose of

Evangelist energy. Good Evangelists recognize those limits in others.

Evangelists find ways to make things happen through others. They are fully aware of the influence they can have on people and take full advantage of it to get *you* working for *them*. Before co-founding Apple Computer, Steve Jobs was a programmer at Atari. Jobs wasn't a great programmer, though, as you wouldn't expect an Evangelist to be. So, Jobs convinced his childhood friend Steve Wozniak, who had a full-time job elsewhere, to do the work for him.

Evangelists are by far the most persuasive of the three core types. Again, what they persuade you to do might be so subtle as to escape your notice. An Evangelist can convince you to get him a cup of coffee without even asking for it. You might not even know why you're doing it. Yet you will feel energized to do it, and fulfilled once you do it. This is a neat thing about Evangelists: you get something out of the deal, too. They get their coffee, you feel happy to have done it.

Communication is About Persuasion

Naturally, Evangelists usually pursue greater causes than obtaining coffee. In the business world, it's all about persuasion. Consider Tony Robbins, the renowned motivational speaker. He's made millions on speaking engagements and books that do little more than re-package common sense approaches to living life better. Now, don't get me wrong, I really like Tony Robbins! I fully subscribe to everything he says, and I know he's had a tremendous positive impact on the lives of so many. But how is it that he can do what he does? Can't anyone write a book that espouses the importance of such seemingly obvious lessons as "figure out your goals in life and work toward them?" Well, yes, anyone can write such a book—and hundreds of authors have—but it takes an Evangelist of Tony's caliber to make a successful endeavor out of it.

What Tony sells is not the concepts or the words in his speeches or books. Rather, he sells *the energy behind it*. When Tony speaks, you—*anybody*—will listen. It helps that he's tall, handsome, and has a strong speaking voice. Image is important, but it's Tony's Evangelist energy that draws you in. It isn't *what* he says, it's *how* he says it that gets you to buy his materials. Non-verbal cues such as body language and facial expressions are more important than the words spoken when it comes to an Evangelist's tools of persuasion. People buy Tony's videos so they can have his energy in their living rooms, motivating them to improve their lives.

And then there's Ronald Reagan. Reagan didn't write most of his own speeches, yet he made the words so much more meaningful than they were in written format. Without a doubt, he had talented speech writers and the written speeches on their own are captivating. But listen to how Reagan delivered them. It's a night-and-day difference. Evangelists animate words with a power to move and inspire. In stark contrast to Tony Robbins, who always stands up and moves around with dramatic hand gestures when he speaks, Reagan delivered some of his best speeches *sitting down* at his desk in the Oval Office, with limited hand gestures, and with no live audience cheering him on. Even in this situation, Reagan's soothing voice, compassion, and contagious emotion delivered an unbelievable amount of energy. Think any politician could deliver a speech as well as Reagan? Consider this excerpt from a speech by Reagan—in 1964:

> "You and I have a rendezvous with destiny. We will preserve for our children this, the last best hope of man on earth, or we will sentence them to take the first step into a thousand years of darkness."

Now imagine Gerald Ford reading that. Missing something, isn't it?

It's interesting to contrast the writing and speaking styles of Mavens and Evangelists. Upon reading Orville Wright's deposition in Chapter 2, you get a sense of who he is and the way he sees the world. It is sufficient to read it and get a sense of the man. The written words of an Evangelist, however, alone do not adequately capture a person's essence.

What is the "energy" that characterizes Evangelists? It's impossible to quantify, but you know when you experience it. Words used to describe Evangelists include charismatic, mesmerizing, energizing, optimistic, positive, driven, and focused.

You know you're dealing with an Evangelist if you feel "talked to" in a one-on-one situation. Often, Evangelists "feel" like personas rather than individuals. You are uncertain whether you are getting the real person or the projected image of the person.

Evangelists communicate best in a group. In fact, the bigger the group, the better, because it's more efficient to speak to many people at once. Evangelists have a way of giving and drawing energy from a crowd of people and like to be the center of attention. They want their platform. Their words are delivered with perfect timing with their audience. As the crowd's energy rises, so does the Evangelist's energy. It's a positive reinforcing loop.

As I wrote in Chapter 2, Evangelists are the most persuasive of the three core types. Evangelists only seek to persuade you to the point at which you are catalyzed to take action. An Evangelist persuades with his personality, passion, and energy, traits you will find contagious. Aristotle called this an *ethos* type of persuasion, which really means that an Evangelist's source of persuasion is himself. Evangelists couldn't care less if you agree with their position. They're not concerned, as Mavens are, with the "rightness" of their argument. However, if you disagree with the Evangelist, you are completely wrong. Be careful debating with an Evangelist; you will lose every time because the Evangelist will convince you that you did, regardless of the merits of your arguments.

Knowledge is Only Useful if Practical

Evangelists acquire knowledge on a need-to-know basis. They consider knowledge useful only if they can parlay it into action. Evangelists feel that their attention should not be distracted by information not directly relevant to their causes. As a result, they might often seem somewhat detached from what's happening around them—unless it directly relates to their cause.

Evangelists are a mile wide and an inch deep. Evangelists are only concerned about the big picture of their causes and want others (Mavens and Relaters) to concern themselves with the details. But because Evangelists don't take the time to study things deeply, when new and potentially useful knowledge becomes available, they often won't know about it. The details escape them and, as they discover painfully, the devil is indeed usually in the details.

Relationships are Opportunistic

Evangelists see people in a binary fashion: you are either useful to the Evangelist or you are not. Everyone an Evangelist meets is potentially useful to advancing his cause. The Evangelist will quickly make the determination whether a person will be receptive to his message but take no action, will be someone who takes action, or will simply not be interested. If an Evangelist doesn't see any potential for productive interaction, he will still take the time to impress the new person but won't follow up. If he sees the potential for a working relationship or some mutual actions to take, the Evangelist will get excited and aggressively follow up.

Because Evangelists are so engaging, they gain familiarity with people easily and quickly. Often, people will feel immediately connected to an Evangelist, through their charm or energy. This feeling is usually not reciprocated by the Evangelist, however. Evangelists are not generally "warm" like Relaters. The troops under the Evangelist General George S. Patton never described him as a pleasant man, yet they admired him.

Part II: The Details

At this point, Evangelist readers can jump to the next chapter. You already got the gist of what we had to tell you in this chapter for the rest of the book to make sense. Spend your limited time finishing this book or advancing your causes. Mavens and Relaters, keep reading. Here's the drill-down you're looking for.

Communication Style

When speaking, Evangelists tend to be dramatic (melodramatic, some would say). They are masters at varying their tone, repeating key phrases, and utilizing pauses in their speech for effect. Martin Luther King, Jr.'s "I Have a Dream" speech might be the best recorded example of this.

Of course, not all Evangelists are equally charismatic. George W. Bush, a very strong Evangelist, obviously lacks the polished speaking abilities or stage presence of other Presidents, especially when speaking extemporaneously. Then again, some Americans prefer his speaking style to that of most politicians precisely because it doesn't come across as a "slick politician."

Evangelists speak in absolutes and extremes, with minimal use of softening qualifiers. It's never "fairly good"—rather, it's great, or it's perfect. But positive, re-enforcing qualifiers are widely used. At Apple, Steve Jobs coined the phrase "insanely great" to describe Apple's technology.

"Yes!" is the Evangelist's favorite word ("absolutely!" is also a winner). Quizzed if the product he is selling can do that, "yes!" is the answer that inevitably returns from an Evangelist, and for good reason: the more people say or hear the word "yes," the more likely they are to take action. A popular book for Evangelist salespeople is appropriately titled, *Getting to Yes*.

Evangelists are highly flexible on how they get their message out. They are always the most engaging in person, but they'll leverage phone calls and e-mails when more efficient. E-mail, in particular, is a great tool for its ability to broadcast messages to large numbers of people, quickly and cost-effectively. Evangelists are masters of distribution lists. But the best medium of all is television. It's no surprise that televangelists capitalize on this, as do Evangelist entrepreneurs who market their products and services through infomercials. The visual medium provided by television is the best way to convey the energy of an Evangelist to millions of viewers or potential customers.

Evangelists over-communicate for effect. Carly Fiorina, the former CEO of Hewlett-Packard, was the company's top salesperson in her early career. During her tenure at HP, she stressed the importance of communicating all the great inventions and capabilities of the company. Evangelists believe you should "tell them what you're going to tell them, tell them, and tell them what you just told them." In other words, over-communicate until the message gets through! And they have the unique ability to repeat the same message to all comers. Returning to the Royal/Dutch Shell example in Chapter 2, if Carly Fiorina or Steve Jobs had been at the helm, it is likely they would have gone on a corporate-wide tour to explain the restated numbers to all their investors, customers, and partners.

When speaking to an Evangelist in person, prepare to be interrupted…a lot. They speak fast, think quickly on their feet, and have a hard time holding back their ideas. They'll interrupt you constantly and actually expect you to interrupt them in return—so go ahead; you won't offend them. Evangelists see conversation as a collaborative exercise, like dancing back and forth.

Innovation

Evangelists' innovative capability comes in finding ways to communicate complex ideas simply. They tell compelling stories that will illustrate their points and find ways to market ideas to others.

Evangelists are rarely the creators of ideas, but they are certainly effective propagators of them. Evangelists lean heavily on Mavens to come up with an idea. Apple Computer provides a potpourri of examples. For instance, although Apple is usually credited with inventing the graphical user interface (GUI) first used in the Apple Lisa and Macintosh computers and later copied by Microsoft's Windows, the GUI was actually perfected by Xerox at its Maven-loaded Palo Alto Research Center. Xerox didn't know what to do with the GUI, but when Steve Jobs saw it he knew he could turn it into a hot product. This vision was only part of the equation. Jobs also knew that he could convince the mass market that the GUI was a better way to interact with a home computer. It's the combination of vision and persuasion that makes Evangelists successful.

Career Choices

It's no accident that some of the most powerful leaders in the world are Evangelists. Evangelists are drawn to positions of power and invariably rise to the tops of all kinds of organizations. It's easy to spot them.

Where else can you find them? Evangelists are happiest in roles that involve:

- *Propagating an idea.* Examples: speakers, trainers, teachers, lecturers, preachers.
- *Selling and persuading.* Salespeople, politicians.
- *Being in the forefront.* CEOs, lead singers or lead guitarists in musical groups.
- *Taking risks.* Test pilots, athletes.

The Evolution of the Evangelist

Evangelists start off in life as something analogous to used car salesmen. Their initial Evangelist interactions seem forced and their convincing feels more like strong-arming to "close the deal." Recipients feel manipulated.

As Evangelists evolve, four things happen. First, they realize that most answers are co-created and they don't need to have all the answers in their back pocket. Rather, they can come to the table with one-half of the solution as long as they know how to find the other half. They slowly begin to allow others' ideas to mix with theirs and in turn soften the extremeness of their convictions.

Second, Evangelists start to seek the best outcomes, not necessarily the ones they see in front of them. This often leads to even more powerful outcomes.

Next, they realize that just because they can persuade others, they should not necessarily always try to do so. There are appropriate times for evangelizing, and the audience has to be receptive. They develop discernment over their Evangelist sword. They seek counsel from Mavens and Relaters. Great Evangelists learn to let themselves be tempered by a strong Maven who sets them straight when the situation has changed. And the Evangelist allows his position to evolve over time.

Finally, the Evangelist learns that not everything is solved by an action, both in his life as well as in dealings with his Relater friends (who just want to be heard). They learn to engage their own emotions when appropriate.

The Limits of the Evangelist

Evangelists have some challenges. Foremost, because of their abilities to influence people, they can lead themselves and people down a bad path. The most extreme examples are Adolf Hitler and cult leaders like Jim Jones and David Koresh. Evangelists can be highly egocentric, lusting for power and forcing others into subservient relationships.

In less extreme examples, Evangelists do not consider the impact of their words on others. They might bulldoze over people without regard for their feelings. In his quest to build the Apple Macintosh computer, for instance, Steve Jobs drove his team members to the point of exhaustion and would often scream abuse at them to get the product delivered on time. (Jobs' style has evolved over the years and he is now said to practice a more effective communication style.)

Evangelists can also become rigidly attached to their causes. It can be tricky, and sometimes impossible, to dislodge the Evangelist from his strongly held position. Sometimes that's a good thing, but at other times an Evangelist's stubbornness gets in his own way. Dave pointed this out to me as we debated changing the term "Connectors" to "Relaters" for this book. From an objective (Maven-esque) point of view, the latter term defines this core type better. Yet I resisted the notion of changing it simply because I was so used to saying "Connector."

Finally, Evangelists' relentless pursuit of their causes can blind them from the truth, or from telling the truth. Worse, they might apply their persuasive skills to convince *themselves* that what they know to be false is actually true. For an Evangelist, there is no such thing as objective truth.

What's Next

Thus far, I've attempted to describe the three core types in depth and pinpoint each of their respective strengths and weaknesses. Chapter 5 compares and contrasts the types and will help you understand your place among them more concretely. In addition, in this chapter I will expand the Framework to include an actionable technique for applying it in many areas of your life.

CHAPTER
5

SYNTHESIS

Twenty years from now you will be more disappointed by the things that you didn't do than by the ones you did do. So throw off the bowlines. Sail away from the safe harbor. Catch the trade winds in your sails. Explore. Dream. Discover.

— Mark Twain, in *Humanity*

The first step to understanding people is always to understand yourself. To that end, I hope the detailed explorations of the three core types helped you identify your type and develop an appreciation of the other two. I also hope you noticed that each of those chapters was written in a different style to give you some texture for the three types.

Knowing the types at a high level is the relatively easy piece of the puzzle. This chapter drills down into the details of the MRE Framework to answer some lingering questions you might have, and begins to illustrate some of its practical applications.

Anchors, Blends, Majors, and Minors

The descriptions of the core types in Chapters 2-4 were archetypal—they depicted theoretically "ideal" Mavens, Relaters, and Evangelists—and of course few people fit these descriptions perfectly. In this context, the term "ideal" does not carry a positive or negative connotation. It is not inherently good or bad, nor is it something you should strive to achieve. It's simply a reference point. I call these ideal types *anchors*. Core types are sticky. No matter how hard you might try to temporarily emulate another type or convert yourself to another permanently, your natural tendency will always be to spring back to your true, authentic nature. You are thus "anchored" to that type for life.

Most people are not anchored at the intersecting points of the MRE Triangle. Rather, most people have what I call a blended type. This means that they are anchored as one core type (which I call the *major* type) but have some minority percentage of one of the other types in their fabric (which I call the *minor*). Recall from Chapter 1 that you cannot have all three core types in your fabric. You can, however, emulate a type that is not in your fabric, a phenomenon discussed later in this chapter.

Clearly, not all Mavens, Relaters, and Evangelists are the same. Even those whose types are identical major/minor blends might seem—and in fact *be*—strikingly different people. Personality plays a significant, though limited, role here. As described in Chapter 1, how we act around others conveys a lot of information about who we are and thus shapes others' judgments about us. This leads to differing opinions about two people with the same fabric. But the link between personality and core type is tenuous. Personality is the *who*, core is the *what*. The more significant driver of perceived differences between two people of the same fabric is that one person might have developed their core more than the other. I'll get to that soon.

Core Confusion

You might think you already know what your core type is, but don't be too quick to label yourself. The seemingly obvious answer isn't necessarily the right one. Throughout our lives, we receive conflicting signals and have certain experiences that cause us to re-examine our core type, conclude that our type has changed, or convince ourselves that we are in fact all three types. When I showed drafts of the first four chapters of this book to some acquaintances, I discovered quite a bit of confusion and interest on this issue. One acquaintance, Lisa, wrote:

> "Now, my initial thought was that I could not possibly be a Maven. It seems to me that I adapt to situations, as opposed to having clear intent—particularly when it involves major life decisions (what career to pursue, etc.). I just sort of happen into situations. Or at least, it's always seemed that way to me. But, I re-read this with the Maven idea in mind, and it sud-

denly strikes me that I might, indeed, have clear intent—but that it's perhaps at a subconscious level.

I don't believe that I consciously connect with people by looking at them in terms of how they fit my master plan. On the other hand, I'm the first one to understand how certain connections can be beneficial in the long run, and often in ways you don't anticipate. In that case, I could say that I am finding patterns or purpose in the connections—as opposed to just meeting people for the sake of it. So, I'm not going into it knowing what purpose the connection will serve, but that it ultimately will serve a purpose.

On the other, other hand, I have lots of relationships. I would say that I revel in the diversity of my group of friends. I've been called a connector by many people; people comment on how many people I know and how many friends I have and how many times I've been a bridesmaid or maid of honor. I genuinely like people, and like making connections, but do a terrible job of staying in touch. I just don't do that. If I'm at the computer and happen to see an e-mail or if I'm in the car and happen to have the phone number, I'll call or write someone, but there is no consistency. I think about people all the time, but don't necessarily talk to them all the time, or even some of the time. One of my dearest college friends moved to Canada and I haven't talked to her in two years. Terrible!

I can also be very persuasive; I'm an Evangelist by profession. But I am not always intent on winning people over to my opinion. I can get people to take on volunteer projects they might otherwise not do and I greatly enjoy trying to build a persuasive case. But, if I'm in a group of conservative people who are talking politics, I typically don't get involved. Some arguments aren't worth having. So, even though I passionately believe a certain way, I don't necessarily spend my life trying to spread the news."

My friend Kate offered these observations:

> "I feel that I share some characteristics outlined in this book, but do not share others. While I throw parties and am a Relater as a mother (as most mothers are), in work and other areas I am completely data-driven, analytic and fact-based. I am really bad about keeping in touch with people (partly due to lack of time) and am terrible about remembering birthdays. I guess I feel like these three categories maybe over-simplify what is inherently complex web of personal qualities. While you think of me as a Relater, I make decisions completely analytically, using *Consumer Reports* or whatever data source seems appropriate. So, I guess I don't feel like a true Relater, though I have some of these qualities."

My friend Cyrus wrote:

> "I'm dying to know what my type is, because I'm the biggest Evangelist on the planet. I'm always selling, and every one of my friends comments on that. Yet people are my life and I have over 12,000 people in my instant messenger program. In school, I was friends with almost everyone, from jocks to band kids, to playwrights, to the nerds. However, I can't stand those who call to say nothing. I want a point. Otherwise, I have ten more calls to return! At the same time, I'm a hundred-percent content to spend most of my days and nights completely alone, thinking, analyzing, and then analyzing more....so, are you *sure* it's not possible to be an incredibly diverse individual that has great traits in all three?"

As the comments from these individuals indicate, identifying your core type is not a quick and easy process. It requires some thoughtful introspection. The tricky part is separating *what* you do from *why* you do it. Lisa occasionally does things with intention, has lots of friends, and is very persuasive. Kate can be nurturing and highly social and is analytical. Cyrus can sell, knows a lot of people, and likes to analyze things. On the surface, then, it would seem that each of them demonstrate aspects of all three core types. Again, the issue here is that *what* they do is not directly linked to *why* they do it. All of us need to be analytical *sometimes*. All of us need to nurture *sometimes*. And all of us need to persuade *sometimes*. In regard to identifying your core type, the question is, *why* do you do those things? Identifying the why—the motivation behind the actions you take—will help you unlock your core type. What we do on a day-to-day basis is a different matter.

Another way core types can be confused is that one's core type can be exaggerated or masked by the presence or lack of specific competencies. I mentioned earlier that it's tempting but erroneous to affix labels to the core types, such as "Mavens are smart," "Relaters are social," and "Evangelists are persuasive." But is it really possible to be an unintelligent Maven, an anti-social Relater, or an unpersuasive Evangelist? Sure, because the specific skills, or competencies, that make one smart, or good at relating to others, or able to sell ice to an Eskimo *must be developed.* Your core type is innate, but unless the competencies that capitalize on the core are developed, your core type might never be expressed. Later in this chapter I will discuss "deepening" as a way to develop your core.

There are many other sources of core confusion. The educational system and your parents, among other factors, play key roles in affecting your perception of your own core. I will discuss these issues in Chapter 7.

Core Permanence

Many people struggle with the notion that a core type is both innate and permanent. It's natural to want to believe that we are each in complete control of ourselves, that we can grow and change of our own volition. The notion of permanence—that there's nothing you can do to change yourself, even if you want to—is understandably discomforting. But I'm not saying you can't change. In fact, over time and through the daily experiences of life, you *do* change, and you change regardless of whether you want to.

This kind of change, however, has nothing to do with your core type. A core type is a predisposition to what drives you the most in life: knowledge, relationships, or action. You are born with this fundamental predisposition and it does not change over time. This predisposition is much like an instinct. Humans cannot unlearn how to do instinctual things like breathe. You can learn how to breathe differently and temporarily breathe unusually (like hold your breath for a minute), but no matter how hard you try to change it, you are programmed to breathe in a certain way and will eventually return to this pattern. In much the same way, you are born with a predisposition toward knowledge, relationships, or action. This is hard-wired in your brain. You can emulate other core types but, just as you will return to your normal breathing pattern, so too will you inevitably return to your core type—your authentic nature.

You can observe the innateness of a core type in a child. A friend's two-year-old son has an interesting habit of quietly sitting under his parents' kitchen table, inquisitively watching the actions of adults around him. In my view, their son is a Maven in development. Another child I know can't stop hugging other children. He's remarkably gentle and kind for his young age. I would place a bet that he's a young Relater.

A perception that your type has changed is usually attributable to your expressing your minor side more emphatically, or more often. Your minor type is expressed in specific situations, or when interacting with certain people. An E-minor, for example, might release enormous Evangelist energy but only for the occasional cause that really excites him. Likewise, the E-minor might allow his Evangelist energy to radiate only when around other Evangelists. Or perhaps you have taken a new job that requires you to tap into your minor energy; E-minor Mavens and Relaters thrown into sales roles often shift toward Evangelist in this situation.

Some people, particularly Mavens, believe that they can intellectualize or actualize a change of core type. They feel they can change core types through mental effort or by behaving in a different way. Here is a revealing transcript of an e-mail exchange between my friend Chris and me on this matter:

Chris: I think that I started off in life as a Maven, and have slowly morphed over time into a Relater.

Bijoy: I'm curious about the moving-to-Relater piece. Is that because at your core you're a Relater, or is that because you've simply realized the importance of relationships? Those are two very different things.

Chris: When I was younger, I focused on learning about things. Now I understand that it's more important to learn about people. Just as a Maven can stockpile knowledge, a Relater can stockpile people.

Bijoy: Yes, but yours is still a Maven's approach to relating. It's not that you are not emulating what Relaters do—which all of us have the capacity to do—it's that your approach is "scientific." A true Relater relies much more on intuition about people (just as a true Maven relies on intuition to learn things). In a sense, they don't know how they do things they do. Someone else could study a Relater and write down the individual steps or study Mavens and document how they invent things. But at the core, there is still something mysterious about the process, both to the individual and to outside observers.

Over time, you inevitably grow into your core type. As you grow wiser with experience and education, you become aware of your type's limitations and try to fill in the gaps by emulating the strengths of other types. This process can confuse you about your type, temporarily, but you will eventually spring back to your true core.

Core Emulation

You might occasionally emulate a core type not in your fabric. A Maven like Lisa, for instance, might temporarily emulate a Relater by making an extra effort to keep in frequent touch with her entire network of friends and business acquaintances. Emulation does not mean that someone actually *changes* his core type or major/minor balance. The emulation happens at a superficial (personality) level, not at your core. It's a change of what you do, not what you are.

In fact, the entire concept of emulation is something of an illusion. I've written repeatedly thus far that your behaviors and your core type are not interchangeable. Indeed, when an E-major/R-minor presents a detailed analysis of a complex problem, for example, a casual observer's conclusion that this person is therefore a Maven is groundless. The single data-point of behavior is consistent with that of a Maven, but alone it says nothing about what makes that individual tick.

Emulation tends to occur in short bursts, which makes it easier to accurately separate the occasional behavior from one's "true" core type. Remember, core types are sticky. Although you can try to emulate other core types, your natural inclination will always be to act your type. If our observer spent some time getting to know the E-major/R-minor character in the preceding paragraph, he would eventually observe that this individual is more intent on taking actions toward a cause than conducting elegant analyses.

We see examples of core emulation all around us. One of the more interesting recent applications is in the proliferation of social, dating, and professional networking websites. These sites claim the ability to create, extend, and leverage personal relationships and are loosely modeled after the connecting abilities of Relaters. However, these sites are actually based on false Maven and Evangelist *perceptions* of the way Relaters work. These kinds of websites are generally the least popular with Relaters because they automate what Relaters do best, and prefer to do, in person. Relaters believe that face-to-face interactions can never be supplanted by technology.

Inter-Type Perceptions

Chapters 2-4 discussed how people of each of the core types perceive themselves. But how do the types perceive each other? Other types are viewed as friends or foes, depending on the circumstances and maturity of the individual.

Younger Evangelists prefer to not be in the company of other Evangelists because there is too much competition for the time and focus of those whom they are trying to persuade. As an Evangelist evolves, he comes to realize that he can learn from other Evangelists and hone his skills.

Younger Evangelists also fear Mavens. The ability of Mavens to shoot holes in the occasionally irrational arguments of Evangelists is a formidable threat to the Evangelist's persuasiveness. Even less evolved Evangelists adapt quickly to Mavens' intellectual challenges, however. In a debate between an M and an E, for example, the Evangelist will progressively assimilate the Maven's arguments and cleverly turn them around against the Maven. The earlier quote from Ronald Reagan during his debate with Walter Mondale exemplifies this.

More evolved Mavens and Evangelists see the value in working together. Mavens need Evangelists to overcome their natural resistance to taking action. Evangelists need Mavens to put their overabundance of energy in check, to keep them honest and on track. Mavens also help Evangelists collect and analyze knowledge, a task with which Evangelists struggle.

Not surprisingly, Relaters like both Mavens and Evangelists, and Evangelists and Relaters get along well. Relaters know that strong-minded Evangelists do not like those who disagree with or challenge them, and therefore Relaters rarely attempt to cross an Evangelist's territorial boundaries. More evolved Evangelists acknowledge that Relaters can provide them with useful feedback and balance. Evangelists' relentless pursuit of the advancement of their causes can lead them to step on people, hurting feelings and damaging relationships. Relaters can help temper this trait of Evangelists, but will do so only if asked (nicely).

Mavens generally downplay the inherent value of Relaters. For most Mavens, Relaters' lack of interest in knowledge and their intense focus on illogical emotions is exasperating. Mavens are frustrated by the immeasurable nature of a Relater's qualities, which can't be qualified or represented as real data. Better evolved Mavens eventually learn, however—either through experience or by study—that Relaters can help them in a variety of ways, from finding like-minded Mavens to helping them disseminate knowledge through personal networks. Mavens discover that they can leverage Relaters who are good connectors to magnify their reach and do the hard work of finding the right people.

To obtain the approval and admiration that Relaters crave from Mavens, better evolved Relaters become chameleons. They are aware of the negative perceptions that some Mavens hold against them and, in response, emulate some of the behavioral traits of Mavens to make themselves seem more similar. If a Relater does this well, Mavens will be more receptive to interacting with him.

Both Mavens and Evangelists frequently underestimate the abilities, cleverness, and ambition of Relaters. Relaters can be highly manipulative precisely because Mavens and Evangelists do not expect them to be. More evolved Relaters work in stealth mode, outside the notice of Mavens and Evangelists, harnessing their power of subtle suggestion and their intimate knowledge of personal networks to get what they want. Relaters' ability to quietly make things happen catches many Mavens and Evangelists off-guard.

Energy and The Power of Two
Thus far I've discussed core types in the context of different kinds of people. It was appropriate to frame the discussion in terms of types of people to help you relate to these concepts more readily. However, the concept of core types is broader than types of people. The three cores represent different kinds of energies. Every person is either energized by knowledge, relationships, or action. People still do have a core type, but this is just another way of saying that they are "plugged into" a specific energy. Each person is in fact a holder and a channel of one or two of those

energies. Organizations, communities, entire nations, and even products have a specific type, or energy, too. All of them are either driven by one of the three core energies, radiate one of those energies, or both.

By re-interpreting core types as energy, I can finally introduce one of the most powerful implications of the Framework. By understanding your type and being able to identify those of others, you can work some magic by pairing yourself with people of complementary energies, both professionally and personally. I call this notion "The Power of Two."

The right pairings actually create *more* energy than either person in a pairing has individually or, more accurately, *thinks* he has. Most people don't know how to access their energies, especially their minor energy. But the right pairings release this suppressed energy. It's as if coupling two people—the right two people—lets each person operate at 100%.

Why were Dave and I such good collaborators on this book? Dave is 80% Maven, 20% Evangelist. I'm the inverse, 20% Maven and 80% Evangelist (see Figure 3). That 60% overlap was more than sufficient for us to understand each other. More importantly, the 20% of non-overlap on either end of the same side of the MRE Triangle was sufficient for us to each bring unique strengths to the collaborative effort. The fact that our positions on the Triangle weren't *too* close together meant that we each brought a large dose of different yet complementary energy to the project.

For this particular project, M and E were the right energies we needed. We didn't need Relater energy to create this book. But for other projects, especially the kind involving many people, a Relater might be far more critical to success than having a Maven onboard. A different major/minor balance (not 80/20) might also be more appropriate for certain types of projects, or at certain points in the project. Writing a book is a task best suited to a Maven, promoting a book through certain channels is more of a Relater task, and selling a book is more of an Evangelist task. Being conscious of the specific energy you need and when you need it can improve the chances of success for any endeavor.

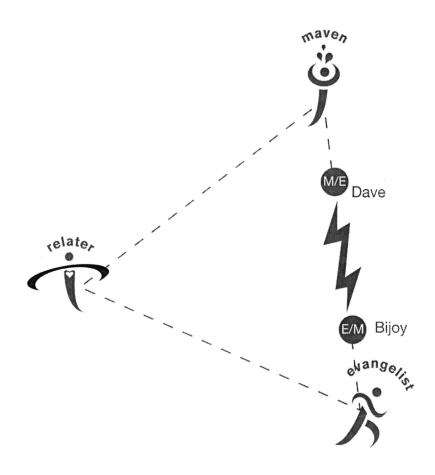

Figure 3:
The Power of Two in a
Professional/Collaborative Context

There is no simple formula for knowing whom you need and when for the myriad permutations of situations in which you might find yourself, but there is a surprising generalization I can offer: the best pairings of people in professional situations tend to be two people whose fabric overlaps on one edge of the Triangle. Dave and I are a case point: we share 60% of one edge. Another viable professional partner for me (though not for this project) would be a Relater who has an E-minor component to their fabric, because in that case we would both possess some Evangelist energy but the partner brings Relater energy that I lack to the mix. I would not have as much professional success working with those who are blends of Relaters and Mavens, since they are not on an edge adjacent to me.

There are numerous examples of this phenomenon in the business world, especially with teams of Mavens and Evangelists who launch technology companies (see Figure 4). For instance, Steve Jobs and Steve Wozniak, both nearly an ideal Evangelist and Maven, respectively, share an edge and were therefore just the right duo to build Apple Computer.

This concept can be applied to shaping social, political, and economic policies, as well. I will discuss this more in Chapter 7, but to spur your thinking on this, ponder for a moment why Silicon Valley spawns so many more successful technology companies than Boston and Austin, the two runners-up. What core type does Silicon Valley have more of than almost any region on the planet?

The Power of Two concept works for personal relationships, too, although the general rule for personal relationships is different than that for professional relationships. For platonic relationships, we seek people just like us. Mavens are naturally drawn to other Mavens, for example. We seek out people of like energy because we don't have to explain our "context" to each other; they understand us at an intuitive level without any explanation required. The fact that we operate in the same way—thought patterns, ways of relating, communication style, and so on—makes the friendship easy and effortless.

Company	Evangelist	Maven
AOL	Steve Case	Marc Seriff
Apple Computer	Steve Jobs	Steve Wozniak
Hewlett-Packard	David Packard	Bill Hewlett
Intuit	Scott Cook	Tom Proulx
Microsoft	Bill Gates	Paul Allen
Oracle	Larry Ellison	Bob Minor
SUN Microsystems	Vinod Khosla	Andy Bechtolsheim

Figure 4:
Technology Companies Founded by Teams of
an Evangelist and a Maven

Think about your own friends—do most of them share your same type? This is not to suggest that you won't have friends anchored at the other types—you will, because you will crave some variety in your life. But chances are that the people with whom you feel the most comfortable and have the longest lasting friendships will have at least some component of your type in their fabric.

For romantic relationships, the adage that "opposites attract" actually works. More precisely, your best personal pairing will tend to be with a partner who is approximately *a length and a half away from you* on the MRE Triangle. Try this! Using a ruler, draw a triangle with three sides of equal length; for simplicity, make each side 1" long. Next, plot yourself on the triangle, and then measure one length and a half (1.5") from that point along the sides of the triangle. As the example in Figure 5 shows, the Framework predicts that an 80/20 M/E would be most compatible in a romantic relationship with a Relater who has a minor component of Evangelist in their fabric. Ideally, this would be close to an 80/20 R/E.

To summarize:

- For working relationships, seek someone proximate to you on the triangle. You want a partner anchored at a different core type but with whom you share an edge of the triangle.
- For platonic relationships, you will generally be happiest with someone similar to you. That is, they should have at least some component of your core type in their fabric.
- For romantic relationships, seek your opposite—a length and a half away from you on the Triangle.

A Recipe for Success

I have hinted that the MRE Framework can be used to help you lead a more fulfilling life. Here is a simple four-step technique to help you do that. I call it the "Four Ds."

1. Discover. As the Oracle of Delphi would agree, the most important thing you need to do to enjoy life is to know thyself. The Framework is a tool to help you understand yourself *better*. It does not provide a complete picture of you, but it does provide a critical foundation and starting point. The Framework is also a tool to help you understand what you're not, and to appreciate the difference.

There are several books which can help you discover yourself. These works focus more on personality than core, but they nonetheless provide valuable insights. Two books, in particular, are worth reading. Marcus Buckingham's aptly named *Now, Discover Your Strengths* takes the reader through a step-by-step process of understanding your talents. *Personality Types: Using the Enneagram for Self-Discovery* by Don Riso is an extremely detailed work that's particularly good for uncovering the nuances of blended types.

2. Deepen. Simply knowing your core type is just the first step, and a relatively small one. The more important step is to deepen your understanding and appreciation of what you are. The word to

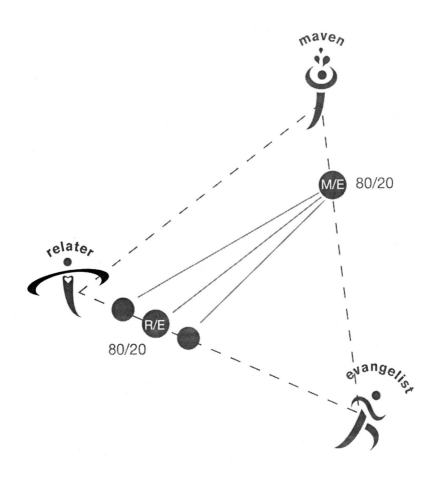

Figure 5:
The Power of Two in a
Romantic Compatibility Context

focus on is *authenticity*. You need to be authentic to your core by dropping value judgments and preconceived notions about the different core types and embracing your particular strengths and weaknesses. Stop trying to emulate the other types and establish a goal to become excellent at *your* type.

If you are an M-major/E-minor, for instance, first accept that you're a Maven and that you have no Relater component to your fabric. Don't try to be a Relater, don't act like one, and don't pursue careers that are best suited for Relaters. Instead, be a superb Maven! Find ways to strengthen your Maven muscle and find ways to inject some of that subdued Evangelist energy into your life.

There are several books which help your type deepen your capabilities. For example, Michael Gelb's *How to Think Like Leonardo Da Vinci* is an excellent Maven guide. *Emotional Intelligence* by Dan Goleman addresses the domain of the Relater. Tim Sanders' *Love is the Killer App* is a manual for Evangelists, written by an Evangelist. Once you know your core, you can guide yourself toward sources such as these to deepen yourself. Spending time building on your weaknesses might be a fun exercise in terms of understanding other types, but not as effective or useful toward focusing on yourself.

3. Dance. Once you identify and embrace what you are, you must also identify and embrace what you're not and actively seek out those energies to round yourself out. Make this a conscious, deliberate process to find a sort of energetic dance partner. If you feel unfulfilled in a certain area of your life, give some thought to which of the three energies you are lacking—and go get it. Feeling unmotivated? You need Evangelist energy. Feeling lonely? You need Relater energy. Feeling mentally unchallenged? You need some Maven. Trust your instinct. When you feel something is missing, it is time to find your energetic complement—your "dance partner."

You will stick with some of your dance partners for various durations. Some will be short term and others will be long term. The latter can lead to some truly incredible results. The Edge and

Bono of the rock band U2 are an example of a long-term, stable partnership of a Maven (The Edge) and an Evangelist (Bono) that has turned U2 into one of the most enduring rock bands of the last three decades.

In contrast, test pilot Chuck Yeager (E) and his project engineer Jack Ridley (M) entered into a short-term and highly effective collaborative partnership with the goal of breaking the sound barrier. Ridley's job was to analyze the streams of data generated during the initial Bell X-1 flights and translate it into things Yeager could do to overcome the technical challenges to breaking the sound barrier. One such problem was a complete loss of the aircraft's elevator effectiveness as the X-1 approached Mach 1. Ridley determined that near Mach 1 the elevator could safely be dispensed with and the X-1's entire horizontal stabilizer, which could be adjusted for trim changes, could be used for pitch control. The idea worked, and Ridley's "flying tail" concept eventually came to be incorporated in all supersonic aircraft. Yeager once said of Ridley: "Jack Ridley knew everything there was to know about aerodynamics and he was practical. And, besides, he was a good pilot...and he fit right in with us. He spoke our language," adding, "I trusted Jack with my life."

Knowing whom *not* to dance with is equally important as with whom to dance. When problem solving or in times of trouble or uncertainty, people default to the modes most representative of their anchor type. For example, when faced with heavy emotional issues, Mavens and Evangelists frequently fall into the trap of pointlessly trying to intellectualize and actualize emotions rather than just *feeling* them. They might want to reach out to someone for help, but the worst person they could reach out to would be another Maven or Evangelist. When facing emotional issues, an M or E should seek a Relater. As another example, if you feel you're not taking action on things you know you need to get done, don't seek the assistance of a Relater or Maven. Dancing with a person of the wrong energy might not help you or, worse, might reinforce your inability to do what is needed.

It is important to acknowledge that it takes a while to become proficient at dancing with a partner. Patience and persistence will be your allies. The first steps are always awkward. Most successful teams—whether professional colleagues or romantic partners—spend years building their relationships before great things result from them. Some of the most successful entrepreneurial teams, in fact, were started by people who had known each since childhood, such as Steve Jobs and Steve Wozniak of Apple Computer, or Bill Gates and Paul Allen of Microsoft.

It also worth noting that finding the right dance partner is not easy. You may need to try dancing with a few different partners until you find the one with the most complementary level of energy. It helps to let everyone around you know that you are looking, and what you are looking for. Your Relater friends can be invaluable in connecting you to potential partners.

Keep in mind that the source of the complementary energies you seek does not necessarily have to be people. There are things all around you that can provide the energy you need. For instance, if you're in a job you loathe, compare your energetic needs with what the employer is providing you. If there's a mismatch, perhaps it's time to find a new job. Geographies radiate a certain energy, too. If you don't feel right where you live, it might be because the energy type of your city or neighborhood does not provide you with what you need. Physical surroundings have a significant impact on how you feel. Consider that advertising agencies, which tend to be full of Relaters, usually have office spaces designed to encourage creativity. Engineering centers, full of Mavens, typically have clean, well organized spaces optimized for efficiency. Certain works of art can flex energy muscles, too. Listening to an emotionally laden piece of music such as opera, or reading an analytical book such as a social science text, can help you tap into other energies.

4. Do It Again. Steps 1-3 represent a continuous process. Once you identify and embrace who you are in Step 1, repeat this step for everyone around you. Seek to understand them, and help them understand themselves. The process of exploring your core with someone who knows you is a wonderfully satisfying experience.

Your mission to deepen your understanding of yourself and others never ends. Returning to the muscle metaphor, if even the most muscular bodybuilder stops exercising, eventually his muscles will atrophy. You need to spend a little effort building up your core muscle every day for the rest of your life.

The dance never ends, either. Although your core type will never change, your energetic needs will vary over time due to your specific circumstances. Get good at trusting yourself about what you need and don't hesitate to seek it out.

Raising the Anchor

How can you best appreciate the world of the other two core types? It all comes back to the anchor. Imagine yourself as a ship, anchored at one point on the MRE Triangle. Even when anchored, a ship can still move around slightly. The slack in the anchor line allows you to experience small variations in the balance of your blended type. If you are anchored at 70% Maven and 30% Relater, for example, you can drift a bit closer to the Relater side (perhaps 35%) or toward the Maven side (75%).

Now imagine what would happen if you raised your anchor. In the MRE Triangle world, you would drift into the center of the triangle. In the center, you free yourself of motivation and stop holding core energy. You, in essence, become neutral. In this state, other people will pull you toward their ship, and your anchor will naturally fall near them. This is a more advanced form of core emulation.

This is a trick that Relaters know about intuitively. Has a Relater ever invited you to lunch, "just to chat?" This request can drive Mavens and Evangelists up the wall. Mavens meet for a reason. They have agendas. They think about what they want to get out of a meeting, whether it's for personal or professional reasons, before it is held. They're on a schedule. Evangelists also have an agenda, but it's always the same one: to drive you to action. The timing doesn't matter—it takes as long as it takes. In stark contrast, Relaters usually don't care about the outcome of the meeting. When a Relater meets someone new, they raise their anchor.

They want the person they're meeting to steer the encounter however he sees fit, because the first conversational steps the Maven or Evangelist take convey to the Relater everything he needs to know about you. Relaters thus deliberately allow themselves to be pulled into the energy realms of Mavens and Evangelists. This is precisely *how* they relate to them so well.

If you are a Maven or Evangelist, you can use this trick to temporarily place yourself in the world of another major type—but it's very, very difficult. Practice this: the next time you meet someone for the first time, say as little as possible while still trying to convey that you are genuinely interested in talking to the person by relying on body language more than words; for example, don't break eye contact, and lean in close to the person. Now, raise your anchor! Turn off the Maven voice in your head running through the mental checklist of "Who is this person?" and "Do I want to know them?" and so on. Abandon the Evangelist urge to try to sign-up this person for your cause. In short, *just let go.* Let them steer your ship and see where it takes you.

Two things will happen with a bit of practice. First, you will develop a keener appreciation of the worlds of the other major types. More valuable, though, is that you will find that you become a more approachable person in the eyes of others. By deliberately *not* radiating your core energy, you cannot repel anyone, as strong ideal types often do. Raising the anchor is a wonderful tactic to openly invite people into your world.

So, What's My Type?

If you haven't yet identified your core type, that's okay! To continue your journey of discovery, visit **www.MREmap.com**. Here, you will find a tool to help you, your family, friends and colleagues jointly discover and declare your MRE profile.

What's Next

Thus far, we've looked at people at the "atomic" level (as individuals, each with a core type) and as simple molecules (combinations of two). Next, we will look at how these atoms and molecules function in a corporate environment.

CHAPTER
6

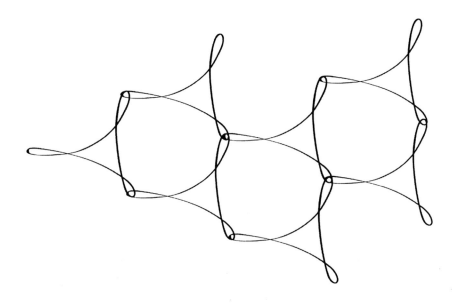

THE MRE FRAMEWORK
FOR CORPORATIONS

The same energies that define the core of individuals also define corporations and the products and services they offer. This chapter describes how to apply the principles of the MRE Framework to understanding corporate cultures and organizational change, improving product development processes, hiring the right people, and building more effective work teams. I only scratch the surface of these topics in this chapter—these issues are so expansive that I will discuss them in greater detail in a separate book.

Corporate Culture, Revisited

The notion that companies have a unique culture has been researched and written about extensively. But what does that really mean? All companies have one thing in common: they are assemblies of people. In fact, the simplified legal definition of a company is "an artificial person." Like people, companies are born, grow, mature, and die. Like people, companies have relationships, with customers, partners, suppliers, and their employees, as well as the communities in which they operate and with political institutions. Companies are similar to people because they are composed of people. And because every person has a core type, an assembly of people will provide a mix of core types that cumulatively define a core type for the entire organization.

Corporate "culture" is thus another way of defining the core type *of an organization*. What does it mean for an organization to have a core type? Recall that in the previous chapter I suggested thinking of a core type as a specific type of energy. Energy flows. If a CEO or Board of Directors has a certain type of energy, it will radiate throughout their organization. It will affect the decisions made by employees, as well as the process by which those decisions are made. In addition, it will affect who is hired and who is not, who the company partners with or acquires, what products are built or services offered, and ultimately who the company's customers are. The core type of an organization is an energy that radiates throughout the company and outward to all of the company's touch points. It is critical to understand that even when an organization is skewed toward one core type, all the types are present—and important.

The core types of the leaders of the organization have the most significant influence over the type of the organization as a whole. This is especially true in a rapidly growing small business, wherein the leaders of the organization are usually the founders. The founders' core type becomes the foundation for the core type of the organization as additional employees are added—and will remain so, until the organization changes its core. The founders will hire people of compatible core energies, and those people will hire the same type, and so on. The rules of arithmetic do not apply in this model; seven Mavens plus three Evangelists in a company of ten people doesn't make a 70/30 M/E organization. Such a balance will, however, tilt the scales toward a Maven organization. The core type of the organization self-perpetuates. Those employees who aren't compatible with the mix (phrased differently, "those who aren't a culture fit") either leave on their own or will eventually be terminated.

Do not confuse core type with core competence. A core competence is what a company does best. As I wrote in Chapter 1, *doing* is entirely different from *being*.

The Maven Organization

Bose Corporation, the loudspeaker and consumer electronics manufacturer, is a classic Maven organization. Its founder and Chairman, Dr. Amar Bose, was an engineer who, while at Massachusetts Institute of Technology, studied why live music sounded richer than music played on home audio equipment. He found that it had everything to do with slight variations in the delay of sound reaching the listener's ears. Loudspeakers in the home sent sound waves directly to the listener, almost in a straight line. But sound waves generated by instruments in a concert hall, for example, reached the listener milliseconds apart because some of the sound generated by the instruments bounced off the walls, floor, ceilings, and furnishings one or more times before reaching the listener. These minor delays and echoes give music more depth and presence. Dr. Bose wanted to mimic this effect in a home environment. He created a company to market his first product, the 901, which was the first loudspeaker to combine speaker components that faced the listener (for a direct sound path) with components that pointed backward at angles (to reflect sound).

The genesis of the Bose Corporation was a Maven solving the very kind of complex, intellectual problem Mavens love to solve. In addition, the 901 loudspeaker was very much a Maven-tailored product. Any discerning listener would appreciate the unique sound it created, but it was also a very technical product with specific and unique technical attributes—and that appealed to Maven consumers more so than Relaters and Evangelists. Bose's marketing reflected the company's Maven culture, Maven product, and Maven customer base.

A Maven organization's mission is, simply put, to be the best in its field. Car manufacturer Porsche typifies this, with its tagline "There is No Substitute." A Maven organization believes that its technical prowess is its key to success. Most technology-based companies fall into this category.

Like Maven individuals, Maven organizations communicate by efficient, often impersonal means. Internally, this means that e-mail is the preferred communication tool. Externally, marketing messages might be delivered through vehicles like infomercials. Notice the proliferation of infomercials, for instance, that emphasize Maven-oriented messages about better, faster, and more efficient products.

Maven organizations tend to be insular. Because they believe their company and its products are superior to anyone else's, they generally do not partner with other companies, preferring instead to "go it alone." They might wait for other companies to approach them about working together. This mentality extends to customer relationships, too; the Maven organization relates to its customers in an indirect and distant manner, because the organization believes it knows what its customers want and therefore does not need to be engaged.

A great attribute about Maven organizations is that they invest heavily both in research and development of new products as well as in their employees' continued learning and intellectual development. Maven organizations understand that their employees need to have cutting edge knowledge and skills to make cutting-edge products.

Maven organizations also tend to be masters at innovation and product-line extensions. Bose parlayed its market position in home loudspeakers to professional loudspeakers, loudspeakers for computers, loudspeakers for cars and boats, noise-reduction headphones, high-tech clock radios, compact music systems, and home theater systems. Bose is now in the process of changing its tagline, "Better Sound Through Research" to "Better Products Through Research," which reflects its expansion into areas other than loudspeakers.

The challenge Maven organizations frequently face is over-engineering and analysis paralysis. Technology-based companies often become too caught up in the technical elegance of their products and forget the customer entirely. Motorola fell into this trap with its previous generation of cell phones. Although the phones packed more ingenious features than any other phone on the market, what consumers really wanted was only a small subset of those features plus customizability. By offering features such as replaceable faceplates and phones in an array of colors, Nokia was able to unseat Motorola as the leader in consumer cell phone market share.

The Relater Organization

Relater organizations are driven to serve their stakeholders—employees, investors, partners, distributors, suppliers, and customers. Customers and employees, in particular, are worshipped. Relater organizations have an obsession with maintaining close relationships with their customers. Although all companies talk about their "customer focus," Relater organizations truly mean it. At these companies, the customer really is always right. One sign of this is that employees are often rewarded, financially and otherwise, for how well they focus on their customers. Most companies in the service sector are Relater organizations, as they have no tangible product to sell—only the service they provide.

Relater organizations emulate large extended families. Employees of Relater organizations love working for their employer because Relater organizations strive to provide an optimal work/life balance for their employees. The software vendor SAS Institute—a blended Maven/Relater organization—promotes a family feel by offering perks such as on-site daycare, a huge cafeteria, and generous vacation and maternity benefits. As the company's CEO, Jim Goodnight, states on the company's website:

> "We've worked hard to create a corporate culture that is based on trust between our employees and the company, a culture that rewards innovation, encourages employees to try new things and yet doesn't penalize them for taking chances, and a culture that cares about employees' personal and professional growth."

Relater organizations do not go to great lengths to make their employees happy just out of kindness—they also believe there are three key tangible business benefits. First, happy employees remain loyal to the company. SAS Institute's turnover is one of the lowest in the software industry. Second, it's a powerful recruiting tool. SAS is consistently rated as one of the best places to work in America, year after year. Finally, more evolved Relater organizations like SAS understand that satisfied employees create satisfied customers.

Unlike insular Maven organizations, Relater organizations embrace other companies in their ecosystem. The retail giant Lands' End is a good example of this; its close-knit relationships with its suppliers are envied, and the company publicly celebrates these relationships. Relater companies excel because of these strong relationships.

Just as Relater individuals prefer personal, high-touch interactions, so too do Relater organizations. Even through seemingly "cold" touch-points as a website, Relater organizations make the user experience personal and comforting, and use every channel they can to convey information about the Relater qualities of the company. Lands' End's website, for instance, has personalization tools with names like "My Virtual Model" and "Personal Shopper," plus sections about the company's history, principles of business, business standards, and corporate giving programs.

Another facet of cultivating a familial culture in a Relater organization is involving all their employees in the decision-making process. Relater organizations make decisions by consensus in a highly collaborative process. Decisions are made in meetings, not by e-mail. Communicating news, whether good or bad, is often done in person by executives, not handed down as a task to mid-level managers.

The Evangelist Organization

Evangelist organizations are on a mission to change the world. Frequently these are companies with cutting-edge technology or a radical new approach to an already solved problem, like Apple Computer's graphical user interface alternative to the IBM-compatible computer, or Amazon.com's goal to conquer the book trade through online sales instead of brick-and-mortar stores.

Most early-stage technology companies are Evangelist in nature, though many transform into Maven companies as they mature. Dell Computer, for instance, would never have gotten off the ground if it weren't for the strong Evangelist nature of Michael Dell, who believed he could produce and market computers less expensively than well entrenched competitors like IBM and Compaq (now Hewlett-Packard). Now that Dell is a multi-billion dollar global corporate giant and computer components have become largely commoditized, Dell has shifted toward a more Maven approach that prioritizes efficient manufacturing and supply-chain management over all else.

The mantra of both working for and with an Evangelist company is, "What have you done for me lately?" Employees are expected to work hard to achieve the company's mission, and those who propel the company closer to its goals are compensated well in exchange. Those employees who cannot carry their own weight are terminated without much remorse. The only standard by which employees are measured is what they have done—not what or who they know. The company's partners are held to the same "sink or swim" standard. Evangelist companies pursue relationships opportunistically, doing whatever it takes to help the company in the short term. As soon as a partner company has outlived its usefulness, the relationship is severed. Quick, decisive, effective action is prized in Evangelist companies.

Communication in an Evangelist company is usually meant to inspire and remind recipients of the goal for which the company is striving. Most so-called "sales-driven cultures" are Evangelist companies. If you've ever worked in a company at which you received a barrage of memos near the end of the financial quarter reminding you that "we're almost there" and "we need everyone to help us reach our targets," you know what working at an Evangelist company is like. Evangelist cultures also tend to encourage internal competition for access to limited resources.

Evangelist companies—almost all of which sell something tangible—have an "it's good enough" approach to product design. Unlike Maven organizations, Evangelist organizations are not as concerned about initial product quality or blockbuster financial results as they are about placing stakes in the ground. Being first to market and capturing large market share, even if by doing it unprofitably or otherwise irresponsibly, is paramount. Microsoft demonstrates this better than any company. The company has historically blundered on its first two or three releases of any new software product, but often scores a home run on the subsequent release. Almost no one bought Microsoft Windows until version 3.1, or Internet Explorer until 4.0, for example. But when Microsoft released the first versions of those products, they signaled to competitors that Microsoft was there to stay—and signaled would-be competitors to stay out. Microsoft also gained valuable real-world usage data on its products and fixed the bugs before making a huge market push for the later versions.

The flip side to this product development approach is that a company might ruin its chances of ultimate market dominance by introducing a string of disastrous products that permanently tarnish the company's reputation. Good Evangelist organizations mitigate this risk by staggering their product launches so that while some products clearly need work, others are market winners, and the net effect is that the company is viewed as good overall.

A bigger problem faced by many Evangelist organizations is overselling, coupled with underdelivery. Evangelist companies like Enron were exceptionally good at selling their vision to investors and the public at large, but couldn't deliver much of what they claimed to have. This phenomenon also devastated quite a few small technology companies as the tech bubble began to burst.

Blended Organizational Types

Like people, companies can have a blended core type. Most larger companies, in fact, are blended. This is because larger companies engage more constituencies than smaller companies. They are typically in more markets, are more geographically dispersed, need to appeal to the investment community, acquire or merge with more companies, and have more partners, suppliers, and customers. The more parties a company interacts with, the higher the likelihood that it will reflect different core energies for specific interactions or goals.

I mentioned the example of SAS Institute earlier, which makes Maven products for Maven customers but internally is run like a classic Relater organization. Another example is the motorcycle manufacturer Harley-Davidson, which is an unusual combination of Evangelist and Relater. The company's products are clearly Evangelist. Its motorcycles are entirely about image, not technical refinement. Harley-Davidson's advertising supports this; its advertisements focus on styling and lifestyle, never mentioning performance, specifications, price, or anything quantifiable that would appeal to Mavens.

The secret to Harley-Davidson's success is not its bikes—it's the strong international community of owners that the company has fostered. Harley-Davidson doesn't worry about the sophistication of its bikes because it really isn't selling machines. What the company sells is an expensive membership in a close-knit community of Harley owners. Harley Owners Groups ("H.O.G.'s") have popped up all over the world and now have over one million members. Their simple mission is "to ride and have fun." In addition, the company offers training on how to ride a motorcycle, sponsors group bike rides and other events nationwide, and even has its own magazine. By building this community—a Relater approach to marketing—Harley-Davidson expanded its traditional Evangelist customer base to include Relaters.

Organizational Change: Core Transition

A critical difference between the core type of an individual and that of an organization is that organizations *can* change their type through deliberate actions, such as by replacing key individuals or establishing new strategic directions for the organization. Organizational change at the core level is a requirement for corporate survival and part of the natural evolutionary cycle. Core transitions are the most challenging thing a company does, and a company is at its most vulnerable while in the midst of this process.

A company should transition to a new core when it falls out of what I call its natural flow state—the somewhat predictable growth and evolutionary patterns shared by most companies. A core change is usually appropriate when things drastically and unexpectedly go terribly wrong—when revenues slump, employee morale plummets, the company's stock price dives, your once loyal customers abandon you. These are indications that a core change might be necessary. The surest sign that a core change is needed is when a company begins to exhibit the darker behaviors of its core (such as Enron, an example I will mention later in this chapter). This means that a particular core orientation has run its course.

Core changes might also be appropriate when circumstances are nowhere near cataclysmically bad, yet the leadership of the company recognizes that it's time to begin a march toward a new core type. Microsoft is an interesting example of this. Microsoft started as a Maven organization, making a simple but elegant operating system. As the company successfully expanded its product line into multiple areas, it became an Evangelist organization that tried to impose its will on the entire software world. This ultimately led to an onslaught of lawsuits by competitors and the prospect of tighter regulation by governments around the world. Microsoft's response was to begin the transition to a Relater organization—in essence, a kinder, gentler Microsoft. The company settled the grievances of its competitors, made some concessions to governments worried about anti-trust issues, and both Microsoft and the Bill and Melinda Gates Foundation have become generous corporate citizens, giving millions of dollars to social causes around the world. An important, and as of yet unanswerable, question is whether Microsoft is actually migrating to another core, or whether this is a skillfully executed game of core emulation. After all, Bill Gates (a Maven/Evangelist) and Steve Ballmer (an Evangelist) are still at the reins of the company and, although they have certainly softened their public-facing tone, they are still the same people. Remember, core types of individuals do not change. Microsoft thus faces an interesting challenge because its leadership does not possess the core energy of its new direction.

Hewlett-Packard is another company going through a transition, but is pursuing the equivalent of a hybrid type. HP was originally a Maven organization, making highly technical Maven-oriented products for Maven organizations, such as scientific testing equipment. Later, as HP began to enter the consumer electronics market—with home computers, digital cameras, and low-priced laser printers—the company migrated toward a Relater position, with marketing messages about how the company's products help consumers connect to their friends and families using the Internet and, of course, HP products. The friendly and supportive culture at HP came to be known as the "HP Way," which embodied a combination of technical excellence with caring for employees and customers. Under the leadership of Carly Fiorina, HP transitioned to adapt dual core natures. While HP's consumer product strategy continues to be Relater-focused, at the corporate level HP is increasingly Evangelist. For example, Fiorina focused heavily on building tighter relations with the investor community and with the media to market HP's energy. HP advertisements now focus less on the products and more on the company. This "dual core" strategy seems to be working well for HP. The Evangelist "buzz" about the company is strong, while the products are well targeted to HP's Relater customers.

There is no simple formula for changing an organization's core type; the process will vary in every culture. Cultural change is a slow process and corporations, like people, are resistant to change. Change must start at the top, with the Board of Directors or the CEO. This is because the Board and the CEO are both responsible for setting the overall tone and strategic focus of the company, which in turn influence every factor that affects the company's core nature. Aligning the people in the organization with the new core type is the tricky part. In some cases, people of one core type must depart from the organization, and people of the desired core type brought in. This is disruptive but might be necessary. A longer-term option is to deliberately begin hiring people of a new core type, gradually replacing those of the former type through attrition. A more radical approach is to spin-off a group from the existing organization. HP did this when it combined and spun-off some of its divisions into a new company called Agilent in 1999. Agilent, which makes highly technical products such as testing equipment and semiconductor components, retains the Maven culture of the old HP organization. By spinning-off Agilent, HP was free to reorganize and refocus on becoming a dual-core Relater/Evangelist organization.

Technology companies in particular tend to follow an E-M-R evolution. Most technology companies are started by an Evangelist, or a pairing of an Evangelist with a Maven. Despite the specific composition of the founding team, technology companies tend to "lean" Evangelist. This isn't surprising, because upstart technology companies tend to introduce new and risky things, and Evangelists are better at overcoming this "risk hurdle" than Mavens or Relaters. As technology companies grow, they tend to become more Maven. This, too, is not surprising; as companies grow, they encounter challenges that are more intellectual in nature, such as how to make the product work reliably, conquer competitors, raise more capital, and penetrate new markets. Ultimately, most technology companies with a consumer-oriented product will shift to a Relater culture as the company attempts to secure the widest possible market appeal and cultivate customer loyalty.

A New Role for Boards

Companies have trouble seeing their own need for core transition. Inertia is blinding. CEOs and other executives become accustomed to the trajectory they've set for their companies and are naturally inclined to believe that they should continue on their current path. They want to stick with what's worked in the past and when times get tough they are too myopic to see that their trajectory will not suffice indefinitely.

Boards of Directors or Advisors can play a critical role in this regard by helping the companies over which they preside by ensuring that the company's core is aligned appropriately, identifying when a core shift is needed, and then helping to manage the transition. Boards should be the overseers of the company's core. They should continuously question whether the company overall—and especially its senior management team—reflects the right core type. Boards already do this to some extent by hiring and firing CEOs to evoke "change." By proactively anticipating changing core orientations and actively guiding the company around the MRE Triangle, Boards can facilitate smoother transitions.

The core types of the Board members must be balanced with the type the CEO. Most companies embrace that a Board should be diverse and contain members from various industries for their breadth of knowledge and experience. I would go further and advocate that the core types of prospective Board members be weighted as a significant factor when considering a candidate. Moreover, while the Board should contain members of all core types, the majority type represented should be either of the types not held by the CEO. The deliberate balancing of core types is the only way for the Board to be able to assess the core alignment of the organization objectively and fairly. If the Board's core type matched that of the CEO, a phenomenon similar to "groupthink" (in which all members of a team lose objectivity and come to the same conclusions) might result.

Core Over-Expression

Whether for an organization or an individual, it is possible to take the characteristic traits of one's core type to an extreme. For an individual, this can turn into a process of self-discovery and can be a healthy way to get to know yourself better. For an organization, if taken too far, this can be disastrous.

As an example, BMW—which has always been a strong Maven organization—may have let its Maven energy drift too far in the last few years. The company introduced a system on all its cars called iDrive, which replaces many of the tactile, ergonomically sound buttons and switches that once controlled the stereo, climate control, and other systems with a video screen controlled by something comparable to a computer's mouse. Though technically impressive—just what you'd expect from a super-Maven organization—the first iteration of iDrive was a disaster in driver usability, which had previously been a hallmark of BMW. Only after years of continuous derision from the automotive press and formerly loyal BMW customers, the company finally started to re-engineer it.

In BMW's case, iDrive wasn't a fatal decision, and in the end the company probably gleaned valuable insight (the hard way) about what its customers value. Other companies weren't so lucky. Enron and Arthur Andersen, two of the best-known financial scandals of recent years, were unable or unwilling to see the darker side of their cores, ultimately leading to their demises.

Enron, an Evangelist company, had an executive team that refused to confront the reality of the company's situation. The company effectively sold its vision to investors but never verified that it could ever realize that vision into which those investors poured billions of dollars. Enron used a complex web of partnerships to hide debt from its accounting statements and deceived investors about its bleak financial situation. At the root of the problem was that the company's Evangelist energy was unchecked and unbridled. It did whatever it could get away with to raise more money to grow. For Enron, a move toward Maven would have benefited the company by helping it distinguish the real from the illusory.

The accounting firm Arthur Andersen was a Relater company that, like most professional service firms, took pride in its trusted relationships with clients. The trouble was, it was so close to its clients that it lost objectivity and resorted to falsifying information to support its clients, and destroying evidence to protect them. Again, a move toward Maven might have helped the company.

Product Design and Innovation

The MRE orientation of a company and of its customers significantly affects the process *by which* products are designed, and the *kinds* of products that are designed. All products appeal differently to each of the core types, and in fact, some products are deliberately optimized for one type.

I tried an experiment at a talk I recently gave. I first asked each member of the audience to determine his major core type. The audience was then divided into three groups, one for each of the types. I then gave each group a vague challenge: design a cell phone. The Maven team worked efficiently and designed a phone laden with features, many of which were based on technologies that did not yet exist—and some that probably never will, like the team's concept of a telepathic phone wired directly into one's brain that transmitted thoughts instead of words. The Maven team employed an iterative, "building block" product development process; one member would suggest a feature, another person would tweak that idea, yet another person would refine it further, and so on.

The Relater team spent more time getting to know each other and talking about the problem than they did coming up with a solution. This team set out to design a cell phone that replicated, as closely as possible, an actual person-to-person conversation. For example, the phone would use live video to show the faces of those conversing, and the phone would be so reliable that it would never drop a call (because that would be rude).

The Evangelist team surprised me. The first thing they did was to redefine the assignment I gave them. They made their goal to design a cell phone that could be brought to market quickly and that would optimize profits. As one team member put it, "This is all about selling more cell phones, after all." (Strange, I thought, because I never said that!) The Evangelist team went on to design a cell phone similar to what I would imagine Microsoft would create for a first release—relatively simple, a little quirky, but probably inexpensive to manufacture and one that could be launched in the marketplace in a short amount of time. Their phone was evolutionary, not revolutionary.

An important lesson from this example is that, given a vague assignment, teams comprising each of the three core types will optimize designs for something different. Mavens universally strive for elegant, sophisticated solutions, regardless of the complexity of the underlying problem. Relaters will strive for the solution that pleases the most and has a personal touch. Evangelists are the wild card. They will often re-define the problem entirely, and then develop a solution to fit.

Equally important as the core types of the people on the product development team is what are the target customer's types (or is—there might only be one type). The core type of the end-user has a material impact on how the product should be designed. For example, I mentioned earlier that Relaters are in touch with the "context" of people. This applies to the products Relaters use, as well. For a Relater, the form of a product is far more important than its function. This is why certain products are so readily embraced by Relaters. Volkswagen's new Beetle is a great example of this. Relaters adore their Beetles as if they were people. Products designed by and for Relaters have personalities. Relaters relate to these machines as if they were people. In contrast, for a Maven, they're just machines.

Apple's Macintosh Computer is another case study in product design for Relaters. Apple designs their products more as pieces of art than utilitarian machines. It's no surprise that Apple wins so many awards for industrial design—Steve Jobs views good design as a fundamental component of the product, not as an afterthought. Beyond just being designed to look good, Apple products are designed to *feel* good when you interact with them, and to make *you* feel good when using them. This is particularly surprising—and impressive—given that Apple is an Evangelist company, yet most of its products, like the Macintosh, are targeted to Relaters.

What about products for Mavens? Mavens prefer elegant technical sophistication. A Maven engineer I know is very impressed with Bowflex home exercise equipment. Unlike most "home gyms" which use blocks of weight to adjust muscle resistance, Bowflex uses steel rods that each have unique tensile strengths, giving each rod a specific resistance level. Instead of adding or removing weights, the user simply pulls on different steel rods. This approach does not work any better than standard weights—five pounds of resistance is five pounds of resistance, regardless of what is generating the resistance—but for a Maven the elegance of one solution over another is an important differentiator. Foremost, Mavens want a high degree of control over their products; the more things they can adjust, the better. In addition, Mavens value efficiency, so a product's ease of use is very important.

Evangelists primarily want one of three things from a product or service: something that allows them to induce action, something that saves time, or something that upholds an image. One of my favorite products is my digital voice recorder. I take it with me everywhere I go. With it, I can capture conversations, personal thoughts, and speeches (including my own). I can then connect the recorder to my computer and e-mail the digitized words to people. Since I communicate better when speaking than writing, this allows me to spread my Evangelist agenda efficiently, and it's a great time-saver, too.

Evangelists want to make bold statements. They do this through everything from the cars they drive to the shoes they wear. Evangelists are, to some extent, the most image-conscious of the three core types. The specific image they attempt to convey is that they are in front of the wave, not riding it—and certainly not behind it. To this end, Evangelists love new electronic gadgets and products that attract attention. You'll find, for example, that many Evangelists sport the newest cell phones, drive sports cars (especially convertibles!), and wear the newest styles of sunglasses. These material symbols connote that the Evangelist is in some way ahead, leading a charge.

Some companies have found ways to make products that appeal to all core types. These are true mass market products. Apple's iPod is one example. Its utilitarian, clean front panel with its small number of clearly labeled, easy-to-use controls appeals to Mavens. Its small size, light weight, and availability in a variety of colors appeals to Relaters. And its hip image appeals to Evangelists. E-mail is another example of a "product" (in this case, really an application of technology) that appeals to all core types. Mavens like e-mail because it allows them to communicate efficiently and with little emotional involvement. Relaters like e-mail because it allows them to easily keep in touch with their network and to broker introductions smoothly. Evangelists like e-mail because it empowers them to spread their message to the masses quickly, effortlessly, and frequently.

The decision whether to "design deep" (tailor a product for one core type) or "design wide" (create a mass market product that appeals to all the types) depends on the marketing goals of the company. Developing a "deep" product is relatively straightforward; simply have a group of the target core type design it, such as Mavens designing a Maven product. To create a mass market product, it's helpful to think of a product in layers. All Apple products look and feel great on the outside, appealing to Evangelists and Relaters, respectively. Inside, the products are technically superb, too, which appeals to Mavens. Many companies try to mask weak underpinnings with flashy exteriors, but such attempts rarely work. Likewise, great products wrapped in an unappealing skin won't sell, either.

I am not suggesting that products targeted to Mavens or Evangelists have no "personality qualities" whatsoever; Porsche cars are designed by and for Mavens and yet certainly have a personality of their own, for example. But that product personality is not human-like. This distinction is important for Relaters, who seek a personal quality to the products they purchase. When Chrysler Corporation was putting the finishing design touches on the Neon, then-CEO Lee Iacocca insisted on an eleventh-hour design change to replace the Neon's rectangular headlights with ovals. He said the oval headlights gave the Neon more of a friendly appearance. They looked like eyes. The marketers picked up on this, and the initial advertising campaigns for the car featured a picture of the Neon's "face," with a caption underneath that said, "Say Hi to Neon."

It is important to understand the very different roles the three core types play in the innovation process. I've discussed some of this in Chapters 2-4. Relaters are variety creators. They excel at identifying all the possible solutions to a problem. Mavens are deep analyzers. They drill into the list of possibilities the Relater identifies, prioritize potential solutions, and solve the best ones. Evangelists are solution propagators. They find problems in need of a solution. Evangelists also find solutions in need of a problem. Evangelists capitalize on the fact that Mavens often come up with terrific solutions to problems that don't seem to exist—but Evangelists have a knack for figuring out what to do with extra solutions.

Job Assignments and Career Paths

Earlier, I listed a few examples of jobs in which Ms, Rs, and Es might be most content. Developing such a list is tricky, because there is a lot of variety within a job title. Consider the title of salesperson. Of course, all salespeople sell *something*. But *how* they sell it and to *whom* makes a big difference in determining if a Maven, Relater, or Evangelist is best suited to the task.

I like to use the example of a real estate agent. Although many agents sell real estate of all types, selling real estate is not a general skill that anyone can do equally well. Consider commercial real estate, such as warehouse space purchased by a distributor. The types of things a commercial buyer will evaluate in such a property are primarily quantitative factors, such as price per square foot, total usable square footage for storage, monthly cost of utilities, and distance to major roadways. The commercial buyer won't be very interested in the building's aesthetics, amenities, or landscaping. Buying most forms of commercial real estate is about keeping costs low and maximizing efficiency. These are precisely the kinds of sales that a Maven agent could make effectively.

Now consider the purchase of a home. Factors such as price and location will still be important but not evaluated in the same objective, number-crunching manner as commercial buyers do. Much more important will be the more subjective elements—the look and feel of the house, the landscaping, the neighbors, the layout, the quality of the school district, and so on. Buying a house is a very emotional process. And Relaters are the best guides through emotional processes.

There is of course another type of house some people buy: a vacation home. Unlike one's typical house where they live at least most of the year, vacation homes are a luxury, not a necessity. Nobody *needs* to have an expensive home overlooking the ocean in which they only live a few weeks of the year. Buying such a house is, to some extent, an irrational purchase. Who better to convince you to spend millions on something you don't need than an Evangelist?

In addition to real estate, you can surely think of dozens of other examples of selling things that would vary by the nature of the sale or the customer's core type. Mavens are best suited to handle sales of technical products to technical (often Maven) customers, such as industrial sales of microelectronic components to an assembler of circuit boards. Evangelists are great at "selling" their companies to venture capitalists to raise money for a risky, unproven technology.

Thinking about matching individuals of certain core types to certain jobs has important implications for hiring decisions. Far too often, employers seeking to fill positions assume that certain skills, like selling or writing, are generic. Alternatively, employers assume that individuals can be equally as competent at a variety of skills. Have you ever seen a job posting looking for an individual who has "excellent analytical skills, outstanding interpersonal skills, and strong persuasive abilities?" Who *wouldn't* want an employee like that? And what candidate *wouldn't* claim to have all three abilities? But how many people really excel at all three? If employers could zero-in on the most important qualities required in a particular role using the Framework as a guide, job postings could be better targeted, more candidates would self-select and only apply for the job that truly fits them, and the interview process could be refined to test whether the candidate actually possesses the necessary qualities.

Every job is primarily conducive to one core type. Matching the right individual to the right job is the first step. Once hired, the task for managers is to help move that individual down the right career path. Many companies make the mistake of forgetting why an individual was hired for a specific role in the first place. The best next career step for Maven hired to do a Maven job should not be in a "touchy-feely" partner-management role. Yet this kind of career pathing happens all the time, because in many companies having a diverse exposure to all facets of the company is perceived as valuable. Of course, all experience is valuable, but putting an electrical engineer into certain sales roles does not benefit the company or the employee if the employee won't succeed at it, nor enjoy it.

To manage an employee's career path, managers need to follow the same "4 Ds" outlined in Chapter 5: discover, deepen, dance, and do it again. In this case, however, the manager must go through this process with someone else, the employee. Once the two individuals have jointly discovered the employee's core type, the manager's goal should be to help the employee evolve both his major and minor core energies further to "sharpen the blade." How the manager does this can be anything from suggesting books that the employee should read, to sending him to training for specific skills, or by giving him certain assignments that "flex the muscles" of his core energy. Finding good partners for him to work with—the dance—is also key. Providing an employee with a mentor who has similar energy but is "further down the road" would also be beneficial.

I cannot stress enough how much the professional "deepening" process needs to be managed carefully. A common mistake authors, lecturers, and off-site group facilitators make repeatedly is assuming that everyone will benefit from their teachings. The Golden Rule doesn't work here. Reading Dale Carnegie's books or attending his organization's lectures on how to be a better speaker or salesperson will not work well for most Mavens or Relaters, for a simple reason: Dale is an Evangelist who created programs for other Evangelists. Intentionally or not, Dale's programs are designed to make Evangelists *better* Evangelists. They are not intended to, nor will, make Mavens and Relaters *into* Evangelists.

Managers can also use the MRE Framework to reward their employees for good work with the specific things that each core type most values. Elizabeth Anders, a manager at the software vendor Symantec, rewards her Maven employees by giving them more training, better tools, and more exposure to smarter colleagues. She rewards Relaters by giving them more face time, higher levels of personal contacts, more flexibility, and an abundance of genuine appreciation. Evangelists are rewarded with the ability to lead their own teams and manage projects.

Regardless of your position in an organization, you should periodically reflect on how closely the organization's core type matches or is compatible with your own, and also on how well your core type matches your specific job duties. Remember that while corporations can change their type, you as an individual cannot. If there is an alignment of types, you will be rewarded for who you are. If, on the other hand, you are out of synch with your employer's core or that of your specific job, your contributions will not be perceived in the way you want them and you will inevitably be disappointed.

Problem Solving and Teams

It is well documented that a team approach to problem solving yields better results than individuals working alone. But it is also true that a team solely comprising members of one core type will produce a very different result than a team solely comprising members of another type, as evidenced in the cell phone design example. Furthermore, a mix of types in a team will produce a different result than a homogeneous team composition, though not necessarily a better one. By understanding this dynamic, the MRE Framework can help managers assemble better teams. The first step is to frame the problem correctly in two interrelated dimensions: the nature of the problem to solve, and the speed at which it needs to be solved versus with how much rigor. Framing the problem correctly dictates the optimal composition of Mavens, Relaters, and Evangelists on the team. It is commonly accepted that the more diverse a team is the better, but this isn't always true.

As a starting point to building the right team, begin with the problem type. As you know by now, Mavens are best at solving complex problems. They can process large amounts of data and draw connections between disparate pieces of information efficiently. They are great at defining strategies, if not tactics. Relaters are best at solving problems that have a human-interface dimension, have an aesthetic component, or require a high degree of creativity. Relaters excel, for example, at marketing and public relations firms with teams dedicated to developing new advertising campaigns. Evangelists are best at solving problems that require extreme "out of the box" thinking or immediate action. If nothing else has worked and your company needs a radical new approach, put an Evangelist on the case.

How soon the team needs to develop a solution might be a more important criterion in some circumstances. Here, hands down, Evangelists will produce the fastest result. By nature, Evangelists will look for a quick, easy-to-implement solution based on what they know works (or think they know). Evangelists work best under a time crunch. Their solution, however, will not be the most carefully thought-out or researched option. It might not even work at all. Mavens, in contrast, will take their time to do the research and craft an elegant solution. It will most likely work, but a company that needs an answer quickly may be bogged down by the Maven team. There are exceptions to this: in 1969, a team of Maven engineers at NASA was under extreme time-pressure to get the troubled Apollo 13 astronauts back to earth, and produced remarkable solutions in short time frames. But it was Gene Kranz—an Evangelist who brought us the phrase "failure is not an option"—who was running Mission Control at the time and directed the work of the engineers. If speed is paramount, a Relater-laden team is not the best approach.

Considering these concepts together suggests interesting approaches to the optimal team composition for various situations. For example, to solve a problem regarding human interaction, load the team with Relaters but make an Evangelist the team leader to drive the problem solving process in a timely manner. Likewise, to develop an aggressive action-oriented plan, load the team with Evangelists but add some Mavens to counter the natural tendency of Evangelists to develop radical, non-viable solutions.

Relaters can play a particularly useful role in almost any team by serving as a liaison with other teams, executives, partners, suppliers, or other parties. Relaters are also naturals at smoothing relations between team members and with external parties. Furthermore, they can inject a dose of creativity into otherwise uncreative tasks. In addition, Relaters are good at coping with a complete lack of structure. Evangelists and, to a lesser degree, Mavens, require a clear mission to their work. In contrast, Relaters thrive on ambiguity. For problems that are open-ended or poorly defined, Relaters can help other team members stay on course and motivated. Furthermore, Relaters fully appreciate the value in working with others and leverage the unique strengths of Mavens and Evangelists. Indeed, Relaters don't know any other way to operate.

Applying the Four Ds

The same process to better yourself can be applied to your company. First, discover the core type of your organization. The bigger challenge is sharing your insight with your colleagues. Even if you're not an Evangelist, emulate one now for spreading the word about your organization's core nature.

Next, help your company deepen its understanding of its core type. The deepening process should involve everyone in the company but must start at the top with the Board and executive team because these individuals set the tone and direction for the entire company. Encourage your colleagues to continuously evaluate what the company is doing against its core nature. Are you hiring the right people to support your organization's core type? Do teams comprise the right balance of core types? Are the core energies of your company's products aligned with the core types of your customers? Framing questions like these in terms of core energies can help put your company on the correct course—and stay on it.

The third step, dance, is about helping your company to seek out and capitalize on the complementary core energies of every organization in your supply and delivery chain. Do your suppliers, distributors, and other partners mirror the same core energy as your company, are they different but complementary, or are they harmfully misaligned?

Understanding your company's core competence can play a useful role in determining what kinds of dance partners your company needs—in short, your company should partner with those firms that are not identical, but complementary to, its core competence. What specific partners your company should dance with, however, should be dictated by complementary core energies.

Finally, do this analysis again and again! Remember: unlike individuals, the core types of companies *do* change. It might happen that once your company discovers and deepens itself, your corporate partners will change, and another opportunity for misalignment occurs. The key is to conduct a periodic corporate self-assessment to determine whether and how things are changing.

What's Next
The first part of the book addressed the fabric of individuals (strands), the Synthesis chapter examined weaving strands together, and this chapter examined weaving those strands into a larger tapestry. The next chapter discusses the ultimate tapestry—the fabric of the world.

CHAPTER
7

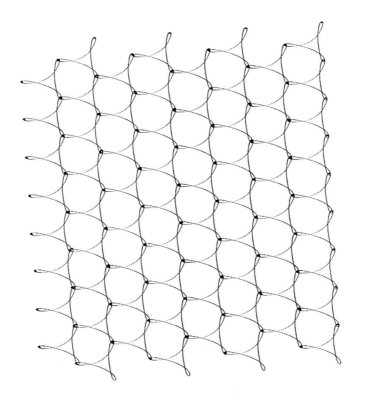

BROADER
APPLICATIONS
OF THE FRAMEWORK

A pplications of the MRE Framework are not limited to understanding yourself and corporations better. The Framework can also be used by individuals, organizations, and governments to make better social, educational, economic, and political policies. This chapter contains my thoughts on how the Framework can help us make sense of the world around us—and how to improve it.

The sections in this chapter are intended merely to call your attention to the myriad of ways in which the Framework can be applied. Each topic is worthy of further research.

Applications for Other Types of Organizations

Chapter 6 examined applying the Framework to corporations. All companies, regardless of size or scope, have one thing in common: their goal is to maximize profitability. This shared goal facilitates generalization of how the Framework applies to companies. But the Framework can be applied to *any* organization, such as government agencies or non-profits—just not as neatly. The following examples illustrate this.

Consider the United States Department of Homeland Security. Its fundamental purpose is Evangelist in nature: to defend the nation, which at times requires mounting a strong offense. This Department has a broader responsibility, though, which is to integrate and coordinate the activities of numerous other agencies and groups involved in national security and disaster relief. This is very much a mission for a Relater organization. Another function of the Department is to collect, analyze, and disseminate intelligence and other information. This, of course, is a task best suited for Mavens. So is this Department Evangelist, Relater, or Maven? It's hard to say. Unlike corporations, government agencies often have conflicting goals and competing agendas that require all three core energies in different areas. This can make ascertaining a government agency's core nature difficult, if not impossible.

NASA is another interesting example. Any space program is inherently risky and decisions regarding it should be based on sound science. Therefore, NASA *should* be a Maven organization from top to bottom. As a government agency, however, NASA cannot avoid being influenced by politicians—especially Evangelists—who pressure the agency not to cancel missions, to cut costs, and to prioritize programs based on political motivations. This can, and has, resulted in disasters.

Some government agencies are easier to analyze. The Central Intelligence Agency, for instance, has always been an Evangelist organization by its very mission. But it was once an organization that depended on Relaters—spies—for "on the ground" intelligence. With the end of the Cold War, the CIA transitioned to a Maven strategy of intelligence gathering via technology, such as through satellite reconnaissance and electronic eavesdropping. With the limits of the Maven approach now apparent, the CIA is returning to a Relater strategy of information gathering through people, not just technology.

Analyzing the core nature of nonprofits can be complicated, as well. Take Greenpeace, for example. Its mission to protect the earth, like that of all environmental groups, is fundamentally Relater in purpose. Greenpeace's close-knit community of volunteers and financial supporters is also Relater in form. But Greenpeace's tactics to evoke change are Evangelist to the extreme. While many environmental groups rely on Maven strategies to evoke change, such as letter-writing campaigns and political lobbying, Greenpeace employs dramatic actions, such as deploying sea blockades using its ships.

Other interesting organizational examples to evaluate would be the Red Cross, Amnesty International, and the Catholic Church.

Education and Parenting:
The Initial Drivers of Core Confusion

The first of the "4 Ds"—discover your core—is not always easy. In Chapter 5, I discussed some of the causes of core confusion, the inability to accurately discern your core type. The two most significant causes are how you were educated and how your parents raised you. I have two goals. First, I hope that understanding how this happens will enable and motivate you to help children (not just your own) discover their core earlier in life. Second, I hope that as parents, educators, and members of society this exploration will help us deepen children's cores from an early age. These goals require an attitudinal change about upbringing, as well as structural reforms to the educational system.

The American public school system—and those in most industrialized nations—is optimized to enhance the skills of Mavens. There is a historic explanation for this. Industrialization is a process that requires the skills at which Mavens excel. Historically, it has been Mavens who have typically spearheaded advances in technology, medicine, manufacturing, and business. (Evangelists and Relaters have of course made important contributions, too, but for right or wrong the contributions of Mavens have often been perceived as greater in significance.) As America moved from an agrarian society to an industrial one, the educational system evolved to reflect the nation's new emphasis on commercial productivity and scientific rationalism. This focus hasn't changed much since the Industrial Revolution. The public school system as it stands is great for Mavens, who revel in logic and facts, but it does little for Relaters and Evangelists. As a result, we have a disproportionate number of people who *think* they are Mavens.

Children legitimately pre-wired as Mavens have a head start in society. Starting in kindergarten, Mavens enter a sort of Maven training ground. Relaters and Evangelists, conversely, reap no specific benefits. What would help Rs is formal training in relationship building, and Es would benefit from training in persuasion and leadership. Yet very few schools, at any level, integrate such training into their curriculum. There are of course some schools, both public and private, with innovative programs and curricula along these lines, but these are the exception, not the rule.

I am by no means suggesting that such basic skills as reading, writing, and mathematics should not be taught to all students, regardless of their core type. I am simply proposing that there are additional courses and activities that would be valuable, and that certain subjects could be taught differently to the various types. Magnet schools—schools that focus on one general subject area, such as math and science or the fine arts—do this well. They still teach all the basic subjects, but the focus, curricula, and teaching methods are better suited to various core types.

In addition to honing students' core types through specific coursework and activities, it is equally important simply to let children know that other core types exist. While many schools teach children about differences in race, religion, and ethnicity, schools generally do not draw attention to the obvious but often overlooked fact that meaningful diversity exists among people of *all* backgrounds. Knowledge about the other core types helps children learn how to relate to other children, as well as with their parents and teachers.   At the most fundamental level, what is missing from most students' educational experience is a guided process of self-exploration. The first time many students are asked to reflect on who they are occurs when writing essays for college applications at age 16 or 17. We unrealistically expect students to choose colleges and courses of study before they've come to understand themselves beyond a superficial level. It's no surprise that the majority of college students change their major at least once. The kinds of materials and programs, such as books and seminars, which can help adults deepen their understanding of their core, are not well suited to a younger generation. In the absence of such materials, the burden falls on parents and society in general to help children deepen their core.

As a society, we tend to presume that college is right for everyone, and that joining the workforce directly following high school carries with it a stigma. For a Maven, more education is almost universally beneficial. But for some Evangelists, staying in school is precisely what holds them back from their natural tendencies.

Parenting also plays a major role in how we perceive our core. Many parents encourage (or force) their children to pursue specific courses of study in school or extracurricular activities. Though their intentions might be good, parents might be encouraging their children to pursue paths that are a mismatch between a child's talents and her core type. They're not the same thing. Just because someone is talented in physics doesn't mean that she is a Maven, any more than serving on student government makes one an Evangelist. But studying math and science extensively, or just being talented at it, can make one *feel like* a Maven. Furthermore, a parent who sees that a child is gifted in math and science might assume that the child is analytical by nature (a Maven) and encourage her to delve deeper into math and science and later attend an engineering school. Many children will blindly follow their parents' guidance. This is why, again, I believe so many college students change their intended major. If we made an effort to help our children identify their core type at an early age, we could then help them develop the specific skills they need to succeed in life.

Economic and Political Policy: Identifying the Gaps

The Framework's third D—dance—can help political and economic policymakers understand why some policies do not work and how to make them work better.

A great example of this is the question of why Silicon Valley produces exponentially more successful technology upstarts than Austin, Texas, which after Boston has the highest concentration of technology companies in the United States. The most obvious explanation is size: Silicon Valley and the San Francisco Bay Area have approximately four times the population of Austin. But Austin doesn't have one-fourth the number of successful upstarts—it has several times fewer than that. Nor is the problem economic. The overall cost of doing business in Texas, especially wages, is far lower than in California, and the amount of venture capital invested in Texas-based companies is disproportionately high compared to Silicon Valley. And the problem is not availability of labor. A large number of Austin area residents are employed in the technical sector, with a diverse range of skills. Moreover, attracting employees to Austin is relatively easy: the overall cost of living is considerably lower than in California, there is no state income tax, and Austin is consistently rated as one of America's most livable cities. Nor is the discrepancy attributable to the fact that Silicon Valley had a head start over Austin. While it is true that Austin's technology sector is younger than Silicon Valley's, Boston has had a technology sector much longer than Silicon Valley has, yet Boston trails it, too.

So what's Silicon Valley's secret sauce? The answer is that while both regions are flush with skilled technical personnel and venture capital, Silicon Valley is also flush with Evangelists, while Austin's technical community is dominated by Mavens. Austin has never had a shortage of great ideas for companies or investors willing to back them. What Austin has lacked is a critical mass of people to bring those ideas to fruition. Austin lacks Evangelist energy all around. With only a handful of exceptions, Austin-based companies lack the ambition to dominate industries globally; they typically do well in niche markets but not on a grand scale.

Austin is an interesting case study because its lack of Evangelist energy permeates more areas than just the technology sector. Austin prides itself on being "the live music capital of the world." The music community in Austin is incredibly strong, with thousands of talented musicians, hundreds of bands, dozens of live music venues, and two nationally renowned music festivals per year. But why aren't many Austin-based bands nationally known? There are several possible explanations for this, but I believe the most compelling one is that Evangelists are missing from the Austin music scene. In the music industry, Evangelists are the people who start record labels, find and produce great bands, and promote artists on an international scale.

Austin is also attempting to become a magnet for the film industry and has made significant progress. Several major film releases were recently shot in Austin, and Austin has a growing pool of talented writers and directors and skilled production crews. With its nascent film industry, however, I believe Austin will hit the same roadblock it has hit with technology upstarts and music. The widespread lack of Evangelists prevents a city—or company, or any organization—from being *outstanding*, settling instead on being, at most, *very good*.

How should Austin attract more Evangelists? First, Austin's City Council needs to understand that its current efforts to spawn a larger film industry in Austin largely impress only Mavens. The City has done a good job of making logical arguments to the industry why Austin is a good place to shoot a film. This has brought filmmakers from other cities to Austin to shoot their films, and then they leave. To catalyze a local industry, the City needs to convince filmmakers to move to Austin, and to encourage those already living there who have Evangelist energy in their fabric to start using it.

Austin needs to appeal to what Evangelists want—an opportunity to make an impact. Austin needs to replicate the excitement and appeal of the gold rush. The "gold" in Austin is the underlying infrastructure already in place to support whatever aspirations Evangelists hold—a large, well-educated labor pool, plenty of money, low costs, and a great place to live. What Austin needs is more people to mine that gold. It's not enough to say that "Austin has potential." The more enticing message to Evangelists is, "Come here, because we need you to capitalize on that potential."

International Cooperation: Finding the Right Dance Partner

I mentioned earlier that entire societies have a specific core energy. Does this mean that societies can, or should, follow the 4 Ds, too? Absolutely! Hong Kong's current industrial development efforts provide a great example.

Hong Kong's government misunderstands its source of economic strength. Hong Kong has a strong Evangelist culture that spans decades, and today its economy is largely driven by shrewd dealmakers and entrepreneurs. Always wanting more, Hong Kong looks to other Asian nations like Japan and South Korea and sees enormous wealth generated by technology firms. After observing the success of these other nations, Hong Kong has decided that it needs to deepen its technological capabilities, continuously "upscaling" its manufacturing and services base toward higher-margin, higher-technology areas, much like Japan and South Korea did over the last fifty years. To this end, Hong Kong is now investing heavily in technical schools and government initiatives to promote technological advancement—in essence, Hong Kong is trying to become Maven.

Hong Kong's approach is not necessarily a bad one, and in fact, its strategy might work in the long run. But there is another alternative, with potentially faster and better results. Instead of trying to emulate another core type, Hong Kong could dance. Singapore would be an excellent dance partner. This city-state is emphatically Maven, and quite good at it. Singapore has an ample supply of technological expertise and high-tech manufacturing capability but, lacking homegrown Evangelists, its technical sector is dominated by foreign firms. The Evangelist energy of Hong Kong coupled with the Maven capabilities of Singapore would make a superb international cooperative partnership.

Lessons from America's Shifting Core

More so than any other nation, America transitions its core repeatedly. At the time of this book's writing, America is Evangelist. This is due, in part, to the fact that a war is in progress—the war in Iraq is very much an Evangelist action, as is the widespread promotion of democracy and market economies abroad—and because President George W. Bush is a strong Evangelist and sets that tone. In contrast, during Clinton's presidency, a time of relative world peace and economic prosperity, America was more Relater. The priorities of the Government and of the people focused more on social programs, foreign aid was heavy, close diplomatic relations were seen as the linchpin to foreign policy over military action, and Clinton set a "friendly" tone for the nation.

America's core nature has also resembled blended types. John F. Kennedy was a Maven who occasionally emulated an Evangelist. His Maven nature is evidenced by his cabinet appointments of intellectuals and the way they analyzed and handled situations like the Cuban missile crisis. But Kennedy's charge for the nation to land a man on the moon by the end of the decade—in part to inspire the people, in part to beat the Russians—was very much an Evangelist action. In response to that charge, America shifted Maven, with thousands of young men and women entering technical colleges to support the space race as well as the defense industry. By the latter half of the 1960s, though, the Vietnam War and domestic social strife drove America to a dual-core Evangelist and Relater nature.

There are some interesting lessons to learn from America's shifting core. The most important one is that America's biggest strength is its adaptability. This adaptability comes from the fact that America is never rigidly anchored to one core. America tends to gravitate toward the midpoints on the MRE Triangle, a position from which it can transition to a new core within a few years rather than in decades. Compare America to the former Soviet Union in this regard. For most of the twentieth century, the Soviet Union operated with an iron fist, with a static Evangelist core. Even after more than a decade since the Soviet Union began to collapse in the early 1990s, it still struggles to shake its rigid Evangelist core and might not do so for years, if ever.

The institutionalized system of checks and balances prevents America from moving all the way to an anchor type and keeps its core blended. It would be impossible in America, for example, for even the strongest Evangelist to hijack democracy and appoint himself a dictator, just as it would be impossible to imagine America becoming so Relater that it dismantles its military in favor of pursuing diplomatic solutions to every world problem. The openness of America's political institutions, with its high degree of transparency, ensures that America does not become "unhinged."

America's frequent elections serve to facilitate core transitions when appropriate. Elections force American voters to reflect on their current core nature and compare it to their desired state. Term limits for some elected officials help keep America's core balanced, as well, by forcing the possibility of new individuals being put in place with different core types.

Corporations can take away two key lessons from America's success. First, there is value in not becoming rigidly attached to one core. Companies that seek to become deep in one core *at the expense of flexibility* cannot adjust quickly enough to changing market conditions. Second, it is valuable to force a periodic re-examination of your core. This applies to individuals, too. Boards of Directors should make an active core assessment an annual event, and individuals should schedule their own annual self-assessment.

Other Areas for Exploration

It is my sincere hope that this book has shown you how powerful the Framework can be in understanding yourself and the people and world around you. But this book only scratches the surface. There are countless other areas not mentioned thus far that are worthy of further exploration, and I hope that some of you reading this now investigate these areas further. I will, too, in future books. To give you some examples:

Health care. Do children diagnosed with attention deficit disorder (ADD) really have a disorder, or are they just frustrated Evangelists trapped in a Maven school system? Are the sources of clinical depression different for Mavens, Relaters, and Evangelists, and should the treatment thus be different for each? Should patients select a doctor based on MRE compatibility?

Psychology and sociology. To what degree is a core type innate versus learned? How can this be proved or refuted? Do the three learning styles (visual, auditory, kinaesthetic) map to the three core types?

Architecture. Do different designs appeal to one core type over another? Can working in specific physical surroundings really improve worker productivity, or boost creativity?

Organizational behavior. How can organizations proactively identify their need for core transition before a crisis necessitates it? How do team compositions of various core types support or hinder problem solving? Can the vague notion of a "corporate culture" be given structure and clarity using the Framework?

Advertising and marketing. Can marketing messages be designed that target customers of one core type while authentically reflecting the core nature of the company if it has a different type?

Political science. Are there patterns in how America's MRE dominance changes over time? What causes these shifts? Can these shifts be predicted?

Moving Beyond the Framework

Bruce Lee was often asked to describe his style of martial arts. He would respond, "I have no style." He believed that when a martial arts practitioner reaches a certain level of skill, he ceases to identify with the particular style of martial arts he has been taught and instead practices "no-style." In every fight, Lee would unconsciously use whatever tactics instinctually felt right at that moment. Rigid adherence to what he had been taught was considered a limitation, not a strength. He learned to let go, to stop thinking and focus on doing, to address situations unconsciously, not consciously.

As you progress on your own journey with the Framework, my hope is that you will eventually employ it with no-style. No-style practitioners of the Framework do not consciously think about the MRE model or run through the 4 Ds. They have developed intuition about understanding core energy. They identify the core types of others quickly and naturally, and then help others deepen their understanding of themselves. They pick dance partners based on gut feeling, not on deliberate analysis—even the Mavens do this! It's like learning to ride a bike; once you get the hang of it, you don't think about balancing, pedaling, turning, or braking. You just do it, without thinking.

Becoming a no-style practitioner of the Framework requires patience, practice, and an open mind. The first and most important step is becoming aware that you and others are unique. Seeing the limitations of the Golden Rule is a sign of your own awakening. Once you see this, you can apply the first D, Discover, to yourself. You must know yourself before you can understand others and the world around you, because *you* are the lens through which all your perceptions will be focused. Once you understand yourself, you can deepen your core and then begin finding dance partners. Start with yourself, then move on to people you care about. Identify a project you've always wanted to work on and challenge yourself to find the right dance partner for it. The first few times you apply the 4 Ds might feel mechanical. That's fine. With time, this will come to be a natural and rewarding process.

I wrote this book to show you a path, but it will only be through your own introspection and interactions with others that you will progress to no-style.

I wish you joy in the process!

APPENDIX:
SUGGESTED READINGS

Works of General Interest

Barabási, Albert-László. *Linked.* Perseus Books Group, 2002.

Buckingham, Marcus and Donald O. Clifton. *Now, Discover Your Strengths.* Free Press, 2001.

Darwin, Charles. *Origin of Species.* Gramercy, 1995.

Easwaren, Ecknath. *The Bhagavad Gita.* Nilgiri Press, 1985.

Gladwell, Malcolm. *The Tipping Point: How Little Things Can Make a Big Difference.* Back Bay Books, 2002.

Lawrence, Paul and Nitin Nohria. *Driven: How Human Nature Shapes our Choices.* Jossey-Bass, 2001.

McCallister, Linda. *"I Wish I'd Said That!": How to Talk Your Way Out of Trouble and Into Success.* Wiley, 1992.

Riso, Don Richard and Russ Hudson. *Personality Types: Using the Enneagram for Self-Discovery.* Houghton Mifflin, 1996.

To Help Mavens Deepen their Core

Michael Gelb has created several books, workbooks, and audio and video programs to help Mavens deepen their core. His book *How to Think Like Leonardo da Vinci: Seven Steps to Genius Every Day* (Dell, 2000) is particularly good for this. See his website for more information: www.michaelgelb.com. Also superb is *Godel, Escher, Bach* by Douglas Hofstadter.

To Help Relaters Deepen their Core

I strongly recommend two works by Dan Goleman: *Emotional Intelligence: Why It Can Matter More Than IQ* (Bantam, 1997) and *Working with Emotional Intelligence* (Bantam, 2000).

To Help Evangelists Deepen their Core

Fisher, Roger et al. *Getting to Yes: Negotiating Agreement Without Giving In.* Penguin Books, 1991.

Sanders, Tim and Gene Stone. *Love is the Killer App: How to Win Business and Influence Friends.* Three Rivers Press, 2003.

For Applying the MRE Framework in Corporations

Buckingham, Marcus and Curt Coffman. *First, Break All the Rules: What the World's Greatest Managers Do Differently.* Simon & Schuster, 1999.

Cox, Jeff and Howard Stevens. *Selling the Wheel: Choosing the Best Way to Sell For You, Your Company and Your Customers.* Touchstone, 2001.

Hargadon, Andrew. *How Breakthroughs Happen: The Surprising Truth About How Companies Innovate.* Harvard Business School Press, 2003.

Watts, Duncan J. *Six Degrees.* W.W. Norton & Company, 2003.

INDEX

LaVergne, TN USA
11 May 2010
182336LV00011B/21/P